WHEN HOT SPRINGS WAS A PUP

WHEN HOT SPRINGS WAS A PUP

Badger Clark

Edited by
Linda M. Hasselstrom and Peggy A. Sanders

©2021 Lame Johnny Press, Hermosa, SD

Copyright © 1983 Linda M. Hasselstrom
Registered July 7, 1983
Copyright © 2021 Fall River County Historical Society/Pioneer Museum

Edited by Linda M. Hasselstrom and Peggy A. Sanders

Introduction, Linda M. Hasselstrom
Editors' Notes, Linda M. Hasselstrom and Peggy A. Sanders
"Requiem for a Cowboy Poet," Peggy A. Sanders
Hot Springs Characters, Badger Clark
Afterword, Slingin' ink and English, Linda M. Hasselstrom
Afterword, A Cowboy's Prayer, Peggy A. Sanders
Additional reading and resources, Linda M. Hasselstrom and Peggy A. Sanders
Chronology, Peggy A. Sanders
Biographies of editors, Linda M. Hasselstrom and Peggy A. Sanders
Additional Photographs – Peggy A. Sanders

Book Design by James W. Parker

All rights reserved.
This book or any portion thereof may not be reproduced or used in any manner whatsoever without the express written permission of the co-editors except for the use of brief quotations in a book review.

Published by Lame Johnny Press, Hermosa SD
First Printing, 2021
ISBN 978-0-917624-04-9

About this copyright

Linda M. Hasselstrom

In 1971, I founded *Sunday Clothes: A Magazine of the Fine Arts* with the help of grants from several agencies, including the South Dakota Arts Council. During the same year, I inaugurated Lame Johnny Press, an independent publishing house which eventually published 23 books; I did not publish any of my own books.

In 1976, while searching as usual for good regional authors whose work I wanted to publish, I discovered that no copyright had ever been registered for Badger Clark's book *When Hot Springs Was a Pup.* The book was originally written for the Hot Springs, South Dakota, Kiwanis Club, and published by the *Hot Springs Star* in 1927. Few Badger Clark scholars seemed to know the book even existed, so, since I had long been an admirer of his poems, I decided to honor the poet and the southern Black Hills by putting it into print.

That first printing of Badger Clark's book *When Hot Springs Was a Pup,* which appeared on July 3, 1976, includes the copyright notice registered to my publishing business, Lame Johnny Press, Associates, Box 66, Hermosa, South Dakota, 57744. The book is paperback, inexpensively printed with a grant from the National Endowment for the Arts through the South Dakota Arts Council. I no longer remember how I met Herb Fisher, once a noted artist with two paintings accepted by Queen Elizabeth for the Royal Gallery in Buckingham Palace. After two years of total blindness, Dr. Fisher's vision had been restored in one eye, and he began recording the late Victorian and Richardsonian architecture of the native sandstone buildings of the Hot Springs area where he lived at the time. He kindly provided black and white sketches and descriptions of buildings for the book. I recently found that first edition advertised for sale at almost $800 online, a sales venue that might have inspired a Badger Clark poem in which he rhymed "online" with "lifeline" or possibly "strychnine." By July 7, 1983, I had learned considerably more about publishing, and chose to close my publishing business so I could spend more time on my own writing.

But I was embarrassed by that first printing, and anxious to present Badger Clark's Hot Springs in a better package, so I reprinted the book with its original foreword by Kennett Harris. Along with the original cover of *When Hot Springs Was a Pup*, drawn by Nigel Havens, and information about him, this edition included many photographs and drawings which had appeared in the original 1927 book, along with new photographs. I included a list of illustrations and a chronology of Hot Springs events taken from Badger's own text. An appendix included a description of Minnekahta Springs from *The Black Hills Souvenir: A Pictorial and Historic Description of the Black Hills* published in 1902, and biographies of both Badger Clark and Kennett Harris, along with an index. I registered the copyright to this edition in my own name, so the registration specifically includes not only Badger's text and Kennett Harris' introduction, but my own introduction to the second and third editions, index and cutlines.

Both copyrights therefore include the complete text of *When*

Hot Springs Was a Pup with Badger Clark as author, along with new materials added to each edition. Included in this fourth edition of *When Hot Springs was a Pup* are my foreword, "Badger Clark's voice long outlives his breath," and my afterword, "Slingin' Ink and English."

Co-editor Peggy A. Sanders owns her "Requiem for a Cowboy Poet," which originally appeared in *Wild West* magazine and concerns Badger's life before he became South Dakota's poet laureate.

An addendum created by both Hasselstrom and Sanders provides additions and corrections to the text, followed by Additional Reading and Resources, a timeline of Badger's life, and an extensive index; all are included in this copyright, as is Badger Clark's "Hot Springs Characters." Any other publication of these materials constitutes a violation of my registered copyrights.

I'd like to think of Badger Clark's words entertaining residents and visitors to Hot Springs for generations to come. Therefore, I hereby grant my copyrights to all of the material in which I have a vested interest in the 2021 edition of *When Hot Springs Was a Pup* to the Fall River County Historical Society/Pioneer Museum, P.O. Box 361, 300 North Chicago Street, Hot Springs, South Dakota, 57747. This gift is intended to allow this nonprofit organization and its nonprofit successors to be the exclusive publishers of legitimate editions of *When Hot Springs was a Pup* in perpetuity.

I believe Badger Clark would enjoy knowing that his words will continue to benefit the historical society in the town for which the book was originally written. As he wrote in "The Last Divide" after hearing his recorded voice:

So thus I may go talking on
After I've seen my final dawn
And partially defeating death
My voice may long outlive my breath
For now the grim old saying fails—
In these days dead men DO tell tales.

Dedication

We dedicate this work to the late
Dave Strain, former owner and proprietor of
Dakota West Books. As a book distributor, Dave
helped so many writers from South Dakota find
readers, and made our books available
throughout the region.

Introduction

Badger Clark's voice long outlives his breath

BY LINDA M. HASSELSTROM

Badger Clark was already famous when he wrote *When Hot Springs Was a Pup* for the local Kiwanis Club in 1927; the little book was likely a fund-raising project.

While Clark's narrative style might seem Victorian to modern tastes, he was a gentleman who respected and even revered "the ladies." My favorite example of his memorable and astute phrasing is a term I use when I am furious in polite company: "Unladylike imprecations!"

Readers may not agree with Clark's suggestion that Hot Springs is a moral town simply because its pioneers were "people of old American stock." While we think history should learn from its past, we suspect not everyone in Hot Springs—or anywhere else—is completely moral. Yet while his comments may appear to be about Indians and white pioneers, they often describe human psychology. Were he writing today, his language would doubtless reflect current usage and ideas.

Part of the purpose of this new edition is so that a new (and perhaps as Badger would say "slackly disciplined") generation may be delighted and instructed. How many writers today can produce such long and convoluted sentences that are perfectly clear as well as deliciously and ironically funny? For his abilities, we will even forgive him for touches of narrow-mindedness, as when he asserts, "The story of the Hills contains material for many poems and novels, for a dozen tragedies and twenty comedies, and for one thundering epic. Someday the Hills will produce the men who can write them." Many women writers were asserting themselves during his time; surely the Badger Clark of today would admit that women write some of those epics.

Historian and author Peggy Sanders and I worked together to create a text that we hope will bring Badger Clark's words to a new audience. We've made no attempt to adjust his opinions to fit the political correctness of the current era. While we would never allow a contemporary author to use the term "squaw," Badger's use reflected the vernacular of his day, familiar to his hometown audience. Likewise, we have left Badger's spelling and punctuation largely untouched, as when he uses "tepee" to refer to a Lakota dwelling, while modern Lakota prefer "tipi."

This edition also contains a biographical sketch of Clark, "Requiem for a Cowboy Poet," by Sanders, including photographs, and a timeline of Badger's life. She also found and provided details on various historical photographs of Hot Springs, including historical photographs by Arundel C. Hull and William Richard Cross, frontier photographers who began their careers in the 1860s.

Contents

Dedication	ix
Introduction	xi
Requiem for a Cowboy Poet	xv
Chapter 1 – Red Rocks and Red Men	1
Chapter 2 – Tepee to Log Cabin	13
Chapter 3 – More Firsts	34
Chapter 4 – Cowboys and Ladies	50
Chapter 5 – The Pup Gets Its Eyes Opened	69
Chapter 6 – Religion, Law and Literature	84
Chapter 7 – Boom!	101
Chapter 8 – The End of the Trail	121
Hot Springs Characters	140
Editors' notes on the text	146
Afterword: Slingin' Ink and English	149
Afterword: A Cowboy's Prayer	159
Charles Badger Clark, Jr. (Badger Clark) chronology	162
Additional Reading and Resources	167
Biographies of the Editors	174
Photographers	176
Photograph and Illustration Index	182
Index	188
Points of Interest	196

Requiem for a Cowboy Poet

By Peggy Sanders

9/28/2017 • WILD WEST MAGAZINE

A foray into colonial Cuba in late 1904 nearly cost Badger Clark, an early day cowboy poet, an indeterminate amount of time on that island—but Yankee ingenuity prevailed. After his release from a Cuban jail, but before receiving official permission to leave the island, he absconded on an American steamship and hightailed it back to the United States. From his in-depth exposure to Spanish he brought home a certain familiarity with the language, a skill he'd later find useful.

Charles Badger Clark Jr., a future poet laureate of South Dakota, took his first breath on New Year's Day 1883 in Albia, Iowa. Friends called him Charlie, though he later went by the old family name Badger to alleviate confusion with his father. Charles Badger Clark Sr. was a Union veteran of the Civil War and a Methodist minister. When Badger was still an infant, his family moved to eastern Dakota Territory, where the Rev. Clark established churches and helped found Dakota Wesleyan University in Mitchell. Six months after the family moved to Deadwood in 1898 to serve another church, Badger's mother, Mary, died of tuberculosis; his older brother, Frederick, had succumbed to the disease four years earlier at age 21. Badger and his father "bached it" until 1901, when the Rev. Clark married schoolteacher Anna Morris, who became Badger's muse. As a teen Clark attended Dakota Wesleyan for a year but just didn't take to college. He wanted adventure—and he got more than he bargained for, along with an education he could not have gotten studying books, in Cuba. In December 1903 D.E. Kerr, a real estate investor and promoter operating out of Chicago and Mitchell, S.D., organized a Cuba-bound colonization effort. The linchpin was a land deal of 9,000 acres in Camagüey Province with plans to develop a ranch. For home sites Kerr had obtained an additional 100 acres in Nuevitas, 45 miles east on a direct railway line.

As often happens in such schemes, promoter Kerr had misrepresented certain facts about the living conditions, and within months the proposed colony fell apart, most of the group returning stateside. Clark stayed on and in July 1904 took a job working for Cuban-American farmer Augustin Rodriguez, who raised registered Berkshire hogs. Feral hogs roamed the property of his closest neighbors, Emilio Barretto and son Enrique, which strained relations, as Rodriguez didn't want his pedigreed hogs mixing with the razorbacks. "[Rodriguez] and [Emilio] Barretto spent most of their time walking around each other with the hair of their backs standing up and their teeth showing," Clark later quipped.

Tensions reached the boiling point when *el patrón* had had Badger cut a fence so the pair could trespass on Barretto land to steal coconuts. When confronted by Enrique Barretto, Rodriguez shot and wounded the younger man. Clark and Rodriguez raced the Barrettos to the Camagüey police station but lost. Thus the authorities charged Rodriguez and held Clark on suspicion. "As we were the only Americans in the place," Badger recalled of their time in jail, "the other prisoners were inclined to be sociable out of curiosity. The policemen were also sociable, as were the fleas, which far outnumbered both policemen and prisoners."

As Rodriguez was half-American, he contacted the U.S. State Department, expecting embassy representatives would quickly secure his freedom. He was mistaken. Once formally charged, he wired his brother in New York to post the required $300 bail, but the cable didn't go through. When he asked his American mother to raise the funds, she solicited all over town but couldn't find a benefactor. Clark then asked a compatriot in Nuevitas to post their bail, but the willing friend hadn't any money to loan.

Clark shared a cell with 17 men. "The massive walls on every side," he wrote, "the brutal guards full of the insolence of authority, the lousy convicts with their ribald songs and unprintable conversation gave me a gone feeling at the pit of my stomach, and for the first time since the trouble I could not laugh."

His first night in jail Clark slept on a brick floor with only his coat as a pillow. The next day he learned that his cellmates lived under a hierarchy led by an elderly con they called *"el*

Presidente," and that he could rent a cot. As food was poor and scarce, coffee was the daily highlight. The prison was stifling. Clark procured old magazines written in English, which he read and reread to keep his sanity.

A week into Clark's stint the jailer put another American in his cell—a young, illiterate, penniless cowpuncher from Texas. An especially harsh judge had sentenced the Texan to a year in prison for drunkenness. He and Clark passed the time together. Badger also tutored a young Cuban prisoner eager to learn English.

Authorities released Clark after two weeks but required he remain in Cuba for six months on bail until his case was resolved. Ultimately acquitted in January 1905, he boarded an American steamship without seeking the blessing of the Yanqui-unfriendly Cuban judicial system. Once back in the United States, he made a beeline for the parental home in Deadwood, where the Rev. Clark continued to pastor the Methodist church.

Badger Clark spent the summer of 1905 with a surveying party in the South Dakota Badlands, where he made little money but restored his soul in the wide-open spaces. On his return to Deadwood in the fall he delved into the publishing profession, landing a job as a reporter with the *Lead Daily Call* in Lead (pronounced "leed"), S.D. Though not particularly challenged by writing about small-town happenings, he enjoyed it. Life was good, even better when he got engaged to Helen Fowler, a classmate from Deadwood High. "I must establish myself in a respectable line," he recalled, "make a respectable amount of money, marry a respectable bride and, in due time, die with a respectable circle of grandchildren around my bed."

By 1908 Clark was living like a cowboy and ready to explore that life in writing.

McGovern Library, Dakota Wesleyan University Archives

Clark was respectable, but his life took a different turn. After a prolonged cough and a visit to the doctor he got the dreaded diagnosis: Tuberculosis. He'd caught it in its early stages, though, and the doctor advised a move to the Southwest, as an arid climate was the sole available "treatment" in that era. He left everything—and everyone—behind in the fall of 1905.

Badger meandered, looking for a place to settle. He first tried Albuquerque, New Mexico Territory, then Bisbee and Tombstone in Arizona Territory. But none offered the peace he required. While mulling where to head from Tombstone, he met cowhand E.K. "Spike" Springer, who thought there might be room for Badger on his cousins' ranch just east of town.

There was, and the circumstances fit Clark as if all had been planned. The Spanish he'd learned in Cuba came in handy living so close to the border. Ranch owners Harry and Verne Kendall put him in charge of a small cattle herd with a short length of fence line to ride and maintain. Though he earned a meager salary, Badger had use of a remote adobe hut, where he lived with dogs, cats and a passel of chickens. Furthermore, his work was hardly strenuous and it occupied only about a day per month. The rest of the time he soaked up the atmosphere and wrote, playing an old guitar and honing his singing voice for entertainment. During occasional visits from old ranch hands Clark would treat them to a meal as he listened intently and watched how they handled themselves. Such cowpokes in turn inspired Badger's poetry, prose and songs. In the interim he "forgot" about his TB, which subsided.

Eager to convey his new surroundings to fiancée Helen Fowler and stepmother Anna Clark, he included poems with his letters to them. Anna appreciated Badger's growing talent as a wordsmith and on his behalf submitted a poem he'd titled "In Arizony" to *Pacific Monthly*. When Badger received a $10 check from the magazine, he decided he'd discovered a viable path to respectability—he'd make his living as a writer. He wrote in the vernacular and spelled phonetically for emphasis. His descriptive phrases painted word pictures cowmen could appreciate and city folks could visualize. "Ridin'" was the poem that launched Badger's career as a poet:

> *There is some that like the city—*
> *Grass that's curried smooth and green,*
> *Theaytres and stranglin' collars,*
> *Wagons run by gasoline—*
> *But for me it's hawse and saddle*
> *Every day without a change,*
> *And a desert sun a-blazin'*
> *On a hundred miles of range.*
> *Just a-riding', a-ridin'— Desert ripplin' in the sun,*
> *Mountains blue along the skyline—*
> *I don't envy anyone*
> *When I'm ridin'.*

Clark remained on the Arizona ranch for four years, during which time his father became chaplain at the Battle Mountain Sanitarium in Hot Springs, S.D. In 1910 the Kendall brothers fell on hard times and could no longer afford to keep him on the payroll, so Badger returned to his parents' home on Eighth Street in Hot Springs. As the senior Clark grew increasingly feeble, Anna turned to junior for help. "[I] set about paying back some of the tender care he had given me when I was a sickly boy," the younger Clark later recalled. "That repayment lasted 10 years and was one of the most satisfying tasks of my life." The Rev. Clark died on June 10, 1921.

Badger remained at home with Anna another four years, until she chose to move into the South Dakota State Veterans Home, a privilege afforded her as the widow of a Civil War soldier. With permission from the state Clark then moved into a small cabin in Custer State Park. On Anna's death in 1937, Badger gained a small inheritance, and with assistance he completed work on his own cabin, which he dubbed the Badger Hole. As it had no electricity, he used a woodstove and an icebox set into a recess in the floor. The resourceful Badger toted water from nearby Galena Creek, chopped his own firewood and relied on an outhouse.

Though the mustachioed Badger was tall, slender and handsome, and female readers sent him mounds of fan letters, he remained a lifelong bachelor. As he explained it, he enjoyed the solitude and was glad he never married. He'd twice been engaged to Helen Fowler, but he thought cabin life might be too primitive for his intended.

Anna, who continually encouraged Badger with his writing, once asked him to compose a cowboy prayer. "I had never really heard a cowboy pray," Badger recalled. "I had heard some of them use some language that had a religious flavor, but generally not in a prayerful spirit. She kept after me however, and so I turned out my most famous work." Though often attributed to "Anonymous," it was Badger who wrote "A Cowboy's Prayer (Written for Mother)," the most widely known poem/prayer in Western circles.

It begins like so:

> *Oh Lord, I've never lived where churches grow.*
> *I love creation better as it stood*

Clark spent his later years writing poetry from his study in the "Badger Hole," the cabin he had built in Custer State Park, South Dakota.

South Dakota State Historical Society Archives

That day You finished it so long ago
And looked upon Your work and called it good.
I know that others find You in the light
That's sifted down through tinted window panes,
And yet I seem to feel You near tonight
In this dim, quiet starlight on the plains.

Many of Clark's poems have been set to music. Such well-known contemporary artists as Bob Dylan, Judy Collins, Emmylou Harris and Michael Martin Murphey have recorded Badger's work, notably "Spanish Is the Loving Tongue," based on the cowboy poet's 1907 work "A Border Affair."

In 1937 South Dakota Governor Leslie Jensen, a longtime friend of Clark's, named Badger the state's first poet laureate (or "poet lariat," as he called himself). The artist was known for both his historical and hysterical tales. His collection of short fiction, *Spike*, takes readers through several escapades with Badger and friends. Whether based in fact or not, his stories are descriptive and engaging. His historical nonfiction *When Hot Springs Was a Pup* relates that community's early years. True to form, humor is a strong point in the book. Badger was also published in *Sunset, Scribner's, Ladies' Home Journal* and other respected (and respectable) national publications, Dakota's favorite poet became a much sought-after speaker for events ranging from rural junior high and high school graduations to women's club meetings and the 1913 celebration of Decoration Day (as Memorial Day was known) at Battle Mountain Sanitarium—the very place his father once preached, which remains part of the present-day Veterans

The Badger Hole, which remains largely as Clark left it on his 1957 death, is open to summer visitors.
Peggy Sanders photo

Administration hospital complex. While traveling the Redpath Chautauqua adult education circuit in the early 1920s, Clark admitted, "I soon discovered that having a group of people at one's mercy was rather fun, and I have done a good deal of talking and reading my own verse since, at one time traveling from Vermont to Los Angeles and from Oregon to Florida on my own jaw, so to speak."

Clark never owned a car. To get around he hitched rides, rode the bus and walked. Once on a lark, on Nov. 16, 1917, he hoofed it to Rapid City, some 60 miles north, in 17 hours. He never did have running water or electricity installed in the Badger Hole. But he was able to scratch by on his earnings from writing and speaking. "I can live on $500 a year comfortably today—even on $400," he once told a reporter. "I can't stand to be in debt and won't be. If I want something and can't pay for it, I do without it until I can. The only thing I have against poverty is that I can't afford all the wonderful books I'd like to have."

Yet the lack of remuneration did concern Clark at times. In a candid June 13, 1934, letter to Methodist pastor and friend Ralph Shearer, Badger wrote: "Don't people realize that writing and speaking is work? And that a few handshakes and 'I-enjoyed-it-very-muches' set pretty light on one's stomach and don't satisfy the grocer at all?"

The Badger Hole remains virtually as Clark left it when he died of throat and lung cancer on Sept. 27, 1957. The cabin within Custer State Park is open to visitors during the summer months. His personal effects—including clothing, flags and multiple pairs of boots—are still lined up in his bedroom. One addition to the cabin—electricity—allows for lights instead of kerosene lanterns. Badger Clark himself is buried in the respectable Evergreen Cemetery in Hot Springs.

Chapter 1
Red Rocks and Red Men

One morning in dateless antiquity a hunting party of pre-Columbian Indians, tribe unknown, were trudging through a picturesque bit of country at the southern edge of the Black Mountains, when they descended into a canyon which had red walls and rim rocks of a peculiar conglomerate. At the bottom

A rock-walled canyon and a quiet stream greeted the Indians as they entered the vale.
John Donnell photo

of this canyon they saw a brawling little mountain stream of beautifully clear water.

The hunters were all afoot, for the simple reason that there were at that time no horses nearer than Europe, and they made for the stream thirstily. The first Indian to drink suddenly raised his head and spat out the mouthful of water with a grunt of surprise. The others rejected their first sip the same way and exchanged glances. The water was sweet and good enough, but it was blood warm.

The sluggish prairie creeks which these wanderers knew were sometimes warmed by the sun in the summertime, but now it was fall, and the buffalo grass was silvery with frost in the early mornings. The Indians discussed the prodigy in wondering gutturals and then, exploring the canyon, found the sources of the stream in many springs which gushed great volumes of warm water from the red earth.

Humans of all colors get a shuddering joy out of a mystery, and the hunters were deeply thrilled, even though they had some suspicions that the devil might be in the thing. Likewise all men like to astonish their wives with their discoveries. Andy Gump's cry of "Oh, Min!" is as old as mankind. So the hunting party immediately returned to their camp a few miles away, and brought their wives, children and worldly goods to the warm springs in the red canyon, where the women were gratifyingly wonderstruck. Among these was an elderly squaw who for several weeks had been tormented by pains in her legs. The medicine man of the band had "treated" her with many incantations to the limit of her Indian endurance, but the evil spirits in her legs had withstood his most clangorous attacks, and she was wretched. The cold air of autumn seemed to make her malady worse, and the last few times the camp moved it had been necessary for four stalwart male relatives to tote her in a buffalo hide swung on poles. In spite of the luxury of this conveyance, she depressed the spirits of everybody within earshot by groaning horribly most of the time, and screaming unladylike imprecations whenever one of her bearers chanced to stumble.

The copious waters of the spring by which the new camp was pitched dropped into a sort of natural bathtub that they had eroded from the red rock, and the old lady's bearers, with the idea of propitiating her, set her down beside it.

No sooner had she touched the pool with a curious hand than she rolled bodily into it, and sat there in water up to her neck, grinning ecstatically, and the others gathered round her in concern, thinking she had suddenly lost her reason. "Warm!" she cackled. "Warm! Wah! My bones have been cold for two moons!" As the dear old soul refused to be lifted out of the warm water, and showered with bad language all those who proposed it, her friends finally left her to soak, so to speak, and went about the work of making camp. Several hours had elapsed and the sun had dropped behind the pines at the head of the gulch, when the men of the submerged dame's family held a council of war and decided to take her out of the water by force, at whatever cost in the way of sounds from her sharp tongue. She abused them collectively as they advanced to seize her, and by the time they had raised her to her feet she was beginning to hit with telling effect at the tender spots in each man's personal history, so her rescuers were minded not only to let her drop back into the water, but hold her head under.

But she suddenly ceased speaking. She exultantly stretched her arms above her head and laughed. Then she pushed the astonished men aside, sprang out of the water and trotted to her husband's tepee like a girl. A quick change to dry buckskins in the tent, and she was out again bustling gaily about the work of getting supper and humming the fag-end of an old war song. Her husband who, poor man! had been boarding 'round among his sons and daughters for two weeks, was delighted, and the rest of the band forgot their suppers in watching in awe the capers of the restored invalid.

"Verily," intoned the medicine man, "verily, a mighty god dwells in the water of the spring, and he has driven the evil spirits out of her legs. Behold what it is to have a wise medicine man who can lead you to the very abode of the gods."

Chemical Analysis	
Water temperature	87 degrees
Total residue	87.9995
Inorganic & non-volatile	4.9160
Otganic & volatile	8.050
Sulphate of sodium	8.824
Sulphate of potassium	3.331
Sulphate of calcium	16.290
Nitrate of magnesium	0.150
Iron susqui-oxide	0.260
Alumia	0.021
Silica	1.830

EvansPlunge.com

Thereupon the medicine man chanted above the spring an invocation which sounded exactly like the chemical analysis of the same waters today given us by the wise men of the State University.

This was the first discovery of Hot Springs, and thus did the red canyon of the conglomerate rim rock become a health resort. Hot Springs was "on the map" long before there were any maps of this part of the world. The fame of the healing waters became known to the very thin population of nomads on the plains, and may have spread as far as the Arikara settlements on the Missouri, two hundred and fifty miles eastward—a vast distance in that day of poor communications.

Time passed, centuries of it. Columbus started west to find a better trade route with India and was disappointed to bump into the shores of a new world. Cortez conquered Mexico. Indians along the Atlantic seaboard began to establish their first contacts with Christianity and rum and gunpowder. Bearing banners of strange devices, explorers pushed into the wilderness of the new continent, claiming everything in sight, and beyond, in the name of His Gracious Majesty This or That.

No white man had come nearer to the warm springs than the Mississippi or the Colorado as yet, but bands of wild mustangs of Spanish ancestry appeared upon the northern plains, and the Indians learned to ride them. This enabled them to enlarge their sphere of action and go into the buffalo hunting business on a large scale, and the plains tribes entered upon their day of prosperity and glory.

As the Indians became able to travel faster and further, more

Big rocks made out of little rocks jut out into the river channel.
W. R. Cross photo

of them visited the red canyon of the warm springs, and the health resort business on this site looked up accordingly.

Their regard for the strange warm waters had a superstitious element in it, so "the canyon walled in with big rocks made out of little rocks" became a religious shrine as much as a watering place.

The buffalo business became so prosperous that it began to attract "Eastern immigration," and the Sioux, a powerful and aggressive league of tribes, emerged from the forests of the Great Lakes Country, learned to ride horseback and, spreading westward, became buffalo hunters, at the same time trampling down and driving out the original possessors of the land in a perfectly civilized and enlightened manner.

One day a band of these Sioux invaders followed the trail of a buffalo herd through the deep pass in the hills near the site of the present town of Buffalo Gap, and a few hours later the warm springs were discovered again. The Sioux, surprised and delighted at the gushing fountains and the limpid stream through the canyon, pitched camp for a long stay. From them we have the first names for the locality which have survived to our day. In their musical tongue they called the springs "Wi-wi-la-kahta," simply "Warm Springs," or "Warm Waters." A few weeks after this first Sioux invasion, a band of Cheyennes, coming to the springs with their sick people as their fathers had done before them, found the strange intruders in possession of the canyon, and were by no means pleased. The old men of the two bands—always the civil authority among Indians—opened diplomatic exchanges in the sign language. The Cheyennes claimed the springs by right of inheritance and

The gap between hills where the buffalo traveled or the buffalo gap.
Peggy Sanders photo

immemorial usage; the Sioux, who, of course, considered their culture infinitely superior to that of the Cheyennes, involved the gods and asserted their right to the place in the name of progress and manifest destiny—an argument which was to be used against them in turn, long afterwards. While the discussion was based on property rights alone, there was some chance of a peaceful settlement, but when the superannuated chieftains on either side warmed to their work and began to shout about national honor, the case at once became hopeless and the young men hastily retired to their respective camps to apply their war paint. As in most international mix-ups, the old men bungled their job of statesmanship and the young men had to pay for it.

The nature of the terrain makes it likely that most of the ensuing fight occurred on the heights now crowned by Battle Mountain Sanitarium, but a battle among mounted Indians always resolved itself into a multitude of single combats and covered a good deal of territory, so there may have been more or less scalp-taking all over the western slope of the mountain whose name preserves the memory of the encounter.

The details of the contest and the number of casualties are lost in antiquity, but tradition says that the battle was long and hot, and that both the day and surviving warriors were worn out when at length the Cheyennes confessed themselves worsted by a sullen withdrawal.

Battle Mountain is the hill on the east edge of Hot Springs. The Battle Mountain Sanitarium, the Veterans Administration (VA), was constructed on the plateau during 1902 to 1907. Fred Evans supplied the locally quarried sandstone.

That evening the Sioux plastered their wounds with mud made of the sacred red soil and spring water, and held a victory dance, but it was not long until they discovered they were not to be left in undisturbed possession of their winnings. It was in the nature of a holy war, and the Cheyennes' religious feelings would not let them leave the shrine of their fathers in the clutches of an enemy after a single defeat. They retired, it is true, but only to make camp in some sequestered nook of the hills unknown to the strangers, whence they returned fiercely to the attack at the most inconvenient times. During the next few days, in fact, the Sioux were so annoyed by the clatter and clamor of Cheyenne raiding parties dashing wildly in among their camp kettles at unholy hours that they realized they could never enjoy their visit to the health resort at all unless they came to terms with the other tourists.

At Sioux initiative a peace conference was called. The men, seated in a solemn circle, smoked red willow bark and delivered long orations. Of course no orator could be understood by the members of the opposite party, but a little detail like that would never discourage a born speech-maker, be he red or white. The military forces of the tribes squatted on either side of the council, each warrior with his bow across his knees and the rawhide rein of his pony in his hand, ready in case the negotiations broke down.

Finally, one elder statesman had an inspiration and, getting on his legs, began to speak excitedly in sign language, which both sides could understand. His idea was beautifully simple—and simply beautiful—and the war worn belligerents made haste to adopt it. They declared the springs under a perpetual flag of truce, and all territory within a certain radius neutral ground, wherein no man should unsheathe a knife or pull an arrow from a quiver.

This undated photo shows the perspective of an elder statesman as he leads a discussion at Hot Springs.

This convention was solemnly ratified with many pipefuls of red willow bark—which is quite as sensible a token of ratification as red sealing wax—and then the Cheyennes moved their camp in and enjoyed their delayed bath. If the ghosts of the young men killed in previous fighting looked down from the Happy Hunting Grounds upon this happy but tardy solution of the dispute, their thoughts may have had an unheavenly tinge, but the whole story of Battle Mountain goes to show that savages conducted their international affairs with quite as much wisdom and hindsight as do civilized folk.

At any rate, tradition says that the treaty was made and, as the history of the United States proves that treaty-breaking was almost exclusively a white man's game, there is reason to believe that this agreement was loyally kept by the simple savages of the tribes. The hard-fighting Sioux won and maintained practical ownership of the Black Mountain country—as Lewis and Clark called it—but, once members of any other tribe reached the neutral ground of the healing water, they were safe there as long as they chose to stay. It is said that even private grudges and vendettas had to be settled outside the sacred zone, and the tribal police sternly suppressed any disorder in the neighborhood of the springs. The council after the fight on Battle Mountain made the canyon forever a place of peace, and the sparkling rapids of the warm creek have never been reddened with human blood since that distant day.

Chapter 2
Tepee to Log Cabin

Probably the Muse of History looked on with wonder at the conquest of Western America between the years of 1849 and 1875. She never had seen anything just like it before. She had witnessed many barbarian invasions, wherein tides of savagery had overwhelmed settled communities, but here the usual program was reversed. The Huns and their like had been purely destructive, professional fighters and pillagers, who left only smoking ruins behind them. The invaders of the West, however, were civilized folk, armed but non-military, fighting only when compelled to, and new farms and new cities sprang up along their trails through the wilderness. But the movement was so swift, so crowded with action and pushed with such fierce energy that it confused the Muse of History, and she rubbed her classic Greek brow perplexedly. "This is too much—too strange—too fast," she complained. "I can't get it. I've never seen anything like it in the five thousand years that I've been recording the doings of mankind. I must do something to get it clear in my head. Perhaps the best way would be to stage a repetition of the whole performance in miniature, and then I'll understand it better."

So, for her miniature stage, the Muse of History picked out the Black Hills, a piece of rich and virgin territory right in the center of the continent, which the main Western migrations had left untrodden and unknown. There she staged her synopsis of that wonderful drama, "The Winning of the West." Her prologue was the discovery of gold on French Creek, just

Canvas-covered wagons traveled in group trains for safety. These prairie schooners were pulled by teams of horses or mules, though often oxen were used.

Library of Congress photo, loc.gov

as the greater play had begun with the nuggets in Sutter's mill race. The first motive, as before, was the white man's love of gold—not a very lovely motive, but seemingly indispensable as a curtain-raiser in all the white man's enterprises.

The action followed swiftly. Act I: the crawling of covered wagons across the plains, while the savage native of the land looked on with bewilderment and rising anger. Act II: Grim war, in which the Indians strike out with blind fury against a fate they cannot understand, while the white men fight coolly and skillfully, knowing exactly what they want. Act III: Social confusion, lawlessness—a brief act but very spectacular. Act IV: The white man's genius for self-government asserting itself— first vigilantes, then courts, closely followed by the school and the church. Act V: The completed conquest—the miners quietly at work in the mountains, the herdsmen in possession of the valleys, the coming of the field and the street, peace and civilization.

In this fashion the great American drama was played for the last time on the stage of the last American frontier, the Black Hills of South Dakota. The story of the Hills contains material for many poems and novels, for a dozen tragedies and twenty comedies, and for one thundering epic. Some day the Hills will produce the men who can write them.

During the first white invasion of the Black Hills country the canyon of the warm springs was off the main trails. Consequently Mother Custer had come into being. Main Street in Deadwood had taken shape among the heaps of washed gravel in the gulch, Lead was beginning to cluster about its Homestake, Spearfish was queening it at the head of her lovely valley, Sturgis was growing about its military post and Rapid City was entrenching itself for commercial

A tepee ring or as Badger Clark called it, a tepee circle, was formed when Indians used rocks to hold down the edges of their conical dwellings. When the people moved on, the rocks remained.

supremacy in its strategic position between the main trails from "outside" and the diggings of the mining district—all this before the first white settler laid the first log of the first house beside the warm creek.

In the sense of being a regular place of human resort, Hot Springs is, of course, the oldest town in this region. Tepee circles—circles of sizeable rocks with which the plains Indians held down the edges of the conical tents—were found by the early white settlers in great numbers on the floor of the canyon, on College Hill, on National Heights and nearly every other level spot near the springs.

Probably one is safe in saying that the place had seldom been without its group of skin tepees for centuries, which would make it a town of sorts. But as a white community Hot Springs is, with the exception of Belle Fourche and the "dam towns," the youngest of the Black Hills cities.

Francis Parkman, Jr. wrote *The Oregon Trail: Sketches of Prairie and Rocky Mountain Life* after his overland journey.

Nobody will ever know just when the first white man set foot in the canyon. The Oregon Trail, not far to the south, had carried considerable covered-wagon travel in the eighteen-thirties and forties. Parkman writes of passing through the southern Black Hills with a band of Oglala Sioux in 1846. The movement on the great Trail increased almost to a traffic jam after the California gold discovery. Later, in the sixties, the Union Pacific laid its rails along the Trail, bringing with it a horde of adventurers and buffalo hunters. It seems more than likely that stray hunting parties from all these thousands of migrants must have stumbled upon the springs, but they left no sign of their visit.

Horatio N. Ross is generally credited with discovering gold near Custer, SD on July 27, 1874.

John Stetter speaks of passing through the canyon with a party in 1874. A band of Sioux, he relates, were here at that time, bathing in the old original rock tub which is still preserved at the Hot Springs House.

Undoubtedly there were a number of casual visits to the

locality by white men in this way, but the visit which led eventually to settlement was made, strangely enough, by H. N. Ross, that heavily bearded prospector who, while with the Custer expedition of 1874, washed out the first pan of auriferous gravel on French Creek and started Black Hills history.

At some time between '76 and '79 Ross, in his wanderings as a prospector, prodded his burro into this canyon. He found no "colors" in the gravel of the creek, so probably the place did not interest him, but he remembered the stream because of the unusual temperature of its water. He mentioned the strange warm creek to several in the Hills, among them Col. W. J. Thornby.

John C. H. Grabill Photo

In the spring if 1879, while Col. Thornby was in this neighborhood with Prof. [Walter T.] Jenny, the noted geologist, he remembered Ross's story and determined to find the warm creek. He finally struck the stream near the Falls and then, as he used to tell so graphically, followed it up the canyon.

Titled "Minnekahta Falls, near Hot Springs," this water flow is commonly known as Fall River Falls and is located four miles east of Hot Springs.

With one hand on his six-shooter, carefully scanning the hills on either side—partly in admiration of the scenery and partly in apprehension of stray Indians—the Colonel threaded the windings of the canyon. He saw nothing alive during the journey, however, but thousands of wild water fowl which were busily swimming and diving in the pools of the stream. Arrived at the present site of the town, he hunted out the springs which were the sources of the creek. Near the big spring where the Plunge was afterwards built, he lopped off the top of a cedar sapling, blazed the trunk, and wrote on the blaze with a lead pencil: "This is my spring. W. J. Thornby." Further, he used to tell of stepping off and staking out an approximate quarter-section which took in the springs in the gulch which is now Minnekahta Avenue.

Whether the Colonel was the actual discoverer of the springs or not, he believed he was, and that belief furnished him a thrill which lasted him for life. He was a man of imagination, and the romance of being a discoverer interested him rather more than the possibility of making a profit out of his discovery. Anyway, he was a mining man, as were most of the men in the Hills at that time, and expected, as four out of five then expected, that his mining property would soon yield him an ample fortune.

On his next visit to the springs he found two squaw men, Joe Larive and John Davidson, building a log house near the spring in the side gulch. They announced, in a matter-of-fact way that they were going to jump his claim and the Colonel, quite satisfied so long as they could not jump his honors as a discoverer, gracefully made them a present of the ground.

During the rest of his life the Colonel never tired of telling of the discovery. For more than thirty years he loved the springs

Minnekahta Avenue circa 1891 shows the Gillespie Hotel on the right. The Hot Springs Hotel is the tall building on the left. Both hotels were constructed in 1890.

and the town which grew up around them with a sort of fatherly affection, and in the end, as he undoubtedly would have wished, he died at Hot Springs, within earshot of the stream.

The next two years after the discovery saw no great rush of white immigration to the ancient Indian health resort. Perhaps two dozen people came and went, or came and stayed, during that time. The land was as yet unsurveyed, but the summer of 1881 found the area of the present town pretty well taken up by squatters. Among them were Ludlow B. Reno and

W.J. ("Bill") Germond. Reno, however, shortly afterwards thought he perceived greener pastures at Buffalo Gap. The Plunge spring and its environs were fleetingly held by Joe Brundschmidt, later proprietor of the Buffalo Gap hotel for many years, but he lacked foresight and traded his right to Joe Petty for a horse valued at thirty-five dollars—which in those days was not a very good horse. The actors in the early scenes of the town's history are few, but the stage is a long distance away and their movements seem dim to a spectator of a later generation.

One point seems clear, however, and that is George Turner's right to the honor of being remembered as the first permanent settler on the town site. Mr. Turner landed here, and stuck, in the year 1879, fixing that year for the beginning of the

The George and Mary Trimmer cabin and home place was just north of the present-day Cheyenne River Bridge on Scenic Road.

white man's town. The second settler to stay put was George Trimmer, who with his Indian wife, established a home down the canyon on the tract still known as Trimmer's Grove. Then John Dennis skidded some logs down Catholicon Peak and built his cabin near Trimmer.

George Trimmer and his wife, Mary Boyer, were the second permanent settlers. He started the first orchard in the county during the 1880s when he planted apple, pear and cherry trees.

The fourth settler was Edmund ("Ted") Petty, who at that time owned most of what is now Lower Town. The group of people represented by these few families were at one time not only all the people on the site of the present town, but probably most of the population of the present county. They were a durable little

John Dennis was the father of the first local bride, Miss Mattie Dennis.
W. R. Cross photo

party, these first whites, and they and their descendants have never been without their influence in the canyon from that day to this.

The first important social event of the town took place in 1881 when Miss Mattie Dennis was married to Mr. George Turner, cowman and "first citizen." A wedding in those days was rather an informal affair. In fact, the difficulty of complying with any formalities at all made it hard to stage so solemn a ceremony with proper decorum.

Fred Evans, Sr. during his days of wheeling and dealing in Hot Springs.

The bride could not be led to the altar because no altar existed, and the clergy were as scarce as electric lights. The nearest justice of the peace was at Custer. He was summoned and came down the thirty-five lonely miles of mountain trail, probably glad to function officially in something more cheerful than the occasional six-shooter case to which he was accustomed. License there was none.

The office of the justice of peace contained no blank forms

which bore the slightest relation to matrimony, so at the conclusion of the rite he scrawled a certificate on a sheet of ordinary writing paper. But time has proven he was a good

Dr. Alexander S. Stewart was an architect and builder before he became a physician.

justice and knew his business. Mr. and Mrs. Turner were duly married and, what's more, they are still married.

It is doubtful if any of these first dwellers about the warm springs thought of the place as a town, but during '81 a group of men in the northern Hills began to consider its possibilities.

They were Evans, Dudley, Stewart and Jennings—names now familiar for so long in the canyon that they seem as much a part of it as the rim rocks. Stewart and Jennings were sent

Dr. R.D. (Rudolph Dickenson) Jennings, his wife Mattie (Curtiss) and their daughter Abbie were the fifth family to settle on the town site.

down on a scouting expedition to spy out the land and, like Caleb and Joshua of old, brought back an enthusiastic report. Steps were taken to organize a company to exploit the springs. In the fall of that year Mr. Jennings bought the log house which had been built near the rock-tub spring by Larive and Davidson, the men who jumped Col. Thornby's claim, and

Sam N. Moses was a drover with the Sturgis and Goodell (S&G) cattle drive from Texas. At various times he was a foreman for the TOT, S&G and Bar T Ranches. When the Fall River Protective Association was founded, Moses was hired as their first livestock detective. Over the years, he was a Fall River County sheriff and a deputy U.S. Marshall.

with Mrs. Jennings, settled there as the fifth family on the town site. Family Number Six was added to the town's slender census in the following spring when Dr. Stewart bought from Joe Petty a partially built log house near the Plunge springs, and filed on the surrounding land. He finished the house, which was a story-and-a-half structure and the most imposing building in town, and moved his family down from Deadwood.

That year the company bought from Ted Petty most of the area now included in Lower Town, and platted it.

The prospect for the sale of lots did not seem brilliant, but the first settlers could not have been American pioneers had they not been optimists. The springs were at that time cut off from the lower flat by the impassable narrowness of the canyon below what is now the junction of Minnekahta Avenue and River Avenue, so it was proposed to divide the coming town into two parts, the upper part to consist exclusively of hotels and bath houses, while the flat should be the town proper.

This early photo shows how narrow the canyon was. The Petty Livery is across Fall River on the left.
Arundel C. Hull photo, Eugene Arundel Miller Collection

About this time the hopeful young city began to be known as Minnekahta, a name it bore until 1886.

Minnekahta soon acquired a post office and a regular mail service. The Sidney-Deadwood Stage Line then passed through Buffalo Gap, and from that point the Minnekahta mail was brought over once a week, on Saturday. The first post office was

Dr. Alexander Stewart's home was located near the site of the Indian bathtub, on the current Minnekahta Avenue.

in Dr. Stewart's big log house at the Plunge site, and by eleven o'clock on Saturday morning all the men in town—eight or ten—would be on hand to receive the mail.

When it arrived and they had read and discussed their letters and newspapers, they would generally stay to dinner with the Stewarts. Fortunately Dr. Stewart had bought out a bankrupt grocery stock before leaving Deadwood, and had it stored in a cave in the hillside; otherwise Mrs. Stewart, despite her instinct for hospitality, might have found it difficult to feed all the patrons of the post office every time they came for their mail.

About this time the town enjoyed the first of a long series of Indian scares. A red-hot rumor blew over the range to the effect that Red Cloud was about to loose a horde of warriors on the scattered settlements.

Chief Red Cloud was an Oglala Lakota leader until his death in 1909 at age 87.

The attack never came, but the hint of it, in those days, was enough to set the village agog, and men out on the trails armed to the teeth, attentively watched the wide horizons for Sioux smoke signals or the whiff of dust which might mean a war party.

There was only one hero of this "war," and he was the boy who, once a week, carried the mail from the stage station at Buffalo Gap to Minnekahta. He was Will Reno, son of the L.B. Reno, already mentioned in this story.

While making one of his regular Saturday trips, Will had delivered his mail and was well on his way back to the Gap, when he noticed a cloud of red dust riding in the still air along the trail ahead. His young friends had talked of nothing but Red Cloud and the battle and massacre for days, so naturally his heart missed a beat or two, and he became all eyes as he slowly advanced. A hundred yards further, and he made out hatless black heads and caught the gleam of a bright blanket. Indians! Will's heart, missing no more beats, went into action furiously, pounding his ribs like the throb of a war drum.

The boy impulsively reined his horse to one side. Then he stopped and, after a longing look up a rocky gulch that wound away toward the hills and timber, reined back on the trail and continued toward his approaching fate.

Weak with terror, slouching deep in his saddle, Will went on until he met the savages—several warriors, sitting on their ponies with the superb balance acquired by riding bareback from childhood, a rattling, paintless government wagon and three or four overladen pack ponies, each carrying a plump squaw and dragging a bumping travois.

The boy saw everything, even to the pinkish dust on their dark faces. They rolled their black eyes at him, one said "How!" in a discourteous grunt, and then—they had—passed by! With a queer mixture of relief and panic, Will drove the spurs into his horse's flanks, and never drew rein until he reached the stage station at the Gap. There, still a little white and shaky, he told his story to a group of men.

"They were harmless," said one man. "They were just taking some sick redskins to soak 'em up at the springs. But son, there's lots of rough country along there. If you were scared, why didn't you duck up a gulch?"

"I—I couldn't," said the boy.

"But why couldn't you?"

Many tribes used the travois, from the French travail, to drag loads that were firmly attached to the poles. A young child was being transported in this photo.

"My father told me," answered Will Reno, "that I must never fool around or get off the trail while I was carrying the mail. What's more, he said he'd lick me if I did."

The incident may not be historically important, but it is a good story for a slackly disciplined generation to think about.

Chapter Three
More Firsts

An event of the year '82 which added an important and permanent attraction to the town's assets was the discovery of Wind Cave. Like the Springs themselves, the Cave is likely to have been discovered several times. The late Ellis T. ("Doc") Peirce, beloved pioneer humorist of the Hills and until his death one of the region's best-known citizens, once recorded

Doc Peirce, seated at his typewriter, gazed out the window as he contemplated another of his columns, which he called sketches.

in his fascinating sketches, "Old Time Trails," that a claim for the discovery of the Cave as early as 1877 had been made by Cornelius Donohue.

Mr. Donohue was well and unfavorably known at that time as "Lame Johnny," and finally closed a career more colorful than creditable when a party of order-loving citizens hanged him to a box elder tree near the creek which still bears his nickname. Lame Johnny's general cussedness, therefore, tends to cast a damp shadow of doubt on his veracity, so we are safe in awarding the honor of the discovery to the later and more respectable claimants.

Wind Cave, with its ninety miles of passages forms a sort of gigantic lung through which great volumes of air are breathed in and out.

This is the hole in the rock where Wind Cave was discovered.

Before the present entrance was opened with dynamite, the narrowness of its throat made the Cave asthmatic, as it were, and its deep-toned wheezing was audible for some hundred of yards. It was this mighty bronchial trouble which attracted the attention of Jess and Tom Bingham as they rode near the spot and, following the sound to its source, the astonished discoverers felt the cold, subterranean air blown strongly into their faces from the black hole among the rocks.

This breathing of Mother Earth excites our wonder even today, and to the men in the remote unexplored gulch, it must have been an awe-inspiring phenomenon. It is not surprising that, as old-timers tell, they galloped back to Minnekahta in a state of stuttering excitement.

Tom Bingham is historically credited with discovering Wind Cave.

In the fall of '82 the first public school was opened in a log house on the Dennis place, Mrs. Helgerson being the teacher.

The equipment was primitive, but that was in keeping with everything about the town as yet. On their way to school the children often saw deer among the pines, and mountain sheep were still quite plentiful, fourteen being counted in one band on the slope of Battle Mountain. The last buffalo seen in town was killed on Evans Heights near the present tourist camp in that year of '82, and furnished jerked meat for a great part of the following winter.

The next year, 1883, was marked by a noticeable growth in the baby city. Several new families came in. The two-story

The first school was held in the John Dennis home.

building just south of the present Gibson Hotel was built by Judge Kohler. It was the first frame building in town, and is the oldest structure still in use.

The Gibson Hotel, also known as the Flatiron Building, was built of sandstone. Judge Kohler built the two-story Iowa House which was the first frame building in Hot Springs. Battle Mountain is the hill on the left.

The route of the Sidney stage was changed so that it came into Minnekahta by way of Cascade, thus literally putting the town on the map. The stage station was at about Sixth Street and River Avenue, and Dr. Stewart, who by this time had homesteaded College Hill and built a home at the top of the bluff, was the agent.

Dr. and Mrs. A.S. Stewart had this home constructed in Hot Springs during 1891. Mrs. Stewart and daughter Mrs. W.H. Stanley posed on the porch.
Wigwam photo

The Deadwood coach reached here at ten in the evening while the Sidney stage came in at two in the morning, and the unfortunate travelers from Sidney were expected to take breakfast here at that hour.

Later in the year a stage was put on from Custer, a change chiefly memorable because it was inaugurated by C.L.

The Deadwood Coach, the last official visit of Supreme Court Justices to Deadwood, in 1889.
John C. H. Grabill photo

("Chris") Jensen, who thus made his entrance into business of the town where he afterwards became famous as a horseman and story-teller, finally serving as mayor of the city.

The first religious service was held one summer Sunday morning in '83, on the ground which is now the property of the Sisters' Hospital.

A number of gypsum rocks strewn about the place offered themselves as seats for the congregation, and certainly no more appropriate setting could be asked than the red, pine-plumed

C.L. Chris Jensen was at the helm of his Cascade Springs touring coach in front of his livery station circa 1891. Jensen later started area telephone companies including People's Telephone & Telegraph of Hot Springs. It was ultimately purchased and became Golden West Telecommunications which is still housed in part of the old stone building at 1510 National Avenue.

W. R. Cross photo

wall of the canyon and the clear waters of the stream at its base. The service was conducted by the Rev. Jesse D. Searles of the Methodist church, and he chose for his text: "Ho, everyone that thirsteth, come ye to the waters."

As this text would hint, Minnekahta already considered itself a spa. The health resort idea was never lost sight of, and the only reason more patients had not been treated was that the pioneer population within a practical traveling radius was very sparse,

The original Our Lady of Lourdes, known locally as the Sisters' Hospital, was conducted by the Benedictine Sisters. It had a capacity of 50 patients. The adjacent building was housing for nurses.
Sanford photo

and, being pioneers, most of them were hopelessly healthy. Dr. and Mrs. Jennings had made the pioneer hotel of the town out of their long, low log house, standing on what is now the vacant space back of the Hot Springs Hotel.

The original bathtub in the rock, partly eroded and partly chipped out by Indians—the very tub in which the pre-Columbian squaw was cured—was still in use, and Dr. Jennings added two more tubs of the same sort and over the whole erected a shed to give privacy to the bathers—which, by the way, was the first bath house.

Here a number of patients, mainly adventurers whose lives of hardship and exposure had brought on the rheumatism, came for treatment, and the results in nearly every case were such as to increase the belief of the Minnekahtans in the curative power of their springs. In one case a man had been

The long building in the center was the first hotel, in the home of Dr. and Mrs. Jennings.
Arundel C. Hull photo, Eugene Arundel Miller Collection

carried to the spring, utterly helpless and horribly swollen with inflammatory rheumatism, and after three weeks of the baths had mounted his horse and ridden away, to all appearances perfectly normal. The Indians, who still brought their sick to this sanitarium of their forefathers, did not believe so long a treatment was necessary. They had faith—perhaps through a dim tradition of the original squaw—that one thorough soaking would cure, and as a rule their faith seemed justified. This southwest corner of Dakota, which up to that time had been attached to Custer County, was in 1883 organized as Fall River county, and Minnekahta was designated the temporary county seat. Sometime later the first really heated political affair which the town had ever enjoyed was brought on by that word, "temporary."

The brick store in Oelrichs was constructed about 1882 for the Anglo-American Cattle Company, which was operated by Harry Oelrichs. The building is under renovation in 2021.

There was a county-seat fight between Minnekahta and Oelrichs when the latter town had grown to a point where it felt strong enough to dispute with the spa for capital honors.

The population was exceedingly thin and scattered, but the inhabitants of Fall River County early acquired a consciousness as a political unit, and made quite a lively use of their privileges then as they do now. Feelings ran high, and the mountains and prairies of the county, accustomed only to such mild noises as the bawling of cattle and the popping of six-shooters, for the first time reverberated to the thunders of political argument.

It was anybody's fight right up to election, and on that fateful day the contending forces got out the vote with a thoroughness which—we hope—will never be equaled in this fair county. So thorough was the work of the workers, in fact, that the total of votes undoubtedly exceeded the total of voters. Of course, this was the first election and the population of the county was a matter of guesswork, but there were dark tales of a heavy migration from Custer County sawmills for the day and each side accused the other of remarkable ingenuity in inventing names which, if shouted through the length and breadth of the new county, would have evoked no answer from any man. The two towns were the only polling places in the county and, at the end of the day of battle, C.S. ("Charlie") Eastman, then a citizen of Oelrichs, brought the ballot box from that place up to the temporary county seat. He and Judge Dudley, of Minnekahta, presided over the final count, so that was straight enough. Minnekahta won by sixteen votes and became the permanent county seat. It is probable that that night

C.S. (Charles Sumner) Eastman was a lawyer. He also served as county sheriff from 1889 to 1901.

Photo courtesy Susan Barrow and Nancy Zumoff.

Jim Sheperd, the man for whom Shep's Canyon is named, resided in that canyon. He was appointed as the first sheriff when Fall River County was formed on November 17, 1883.

Minnekahta's canyon walls echoed with wild yells and festive gunpowder, and that the supply of alcoholic stimulants ran so low as to make thoughtful citizens apprehensive of several deaths from snakebite before the town's medicine chest could be replenished.

Men took their politics seriously in those days.

While on the subject of political irregularities, we might break the chronology to tell of an incident which occurred at the first Democratic county convention at Minnekahta in 1884. A little discussion arose as to the nomination for sheriff. Wearing the sheriff's star at that time was a man named Jim Sheperd, whose popularity is made clear by the fact that he was generally known as "Old Shep."

"Old Shep," said one delegate, "is a good man even if he ain't a Democrat. What's the use of nominating anybody else?"

The propriety of such a suggestion was instantly questioned

by some stickler, and the matter finally came to a rising vote, which was a tie. W. F. ("Bill") Wyatt, pioneer ranchman and still a prominent citizen of the county, who was then a young cowpuncher in his teens, had sauntered into the meeting out of curiosity and sat quietly watching the proceedings.

"Here, sonny," said one of the delegates to Wyatt, "Ain't you for Old Shep? R'ar up!"

The cowboy, anxious to please, obligingly rose on his spurred bootheels, with the result that a Republican was nominated on the Democratic ticket by the vote of a minor.

Equally irregular is a story told of Frank Callahan, the first coroner of the county. A range rider one day discovered on the bank of Horsehead Creek the body of a man who had evidently met death by drowning. The rider summoned people from the nearest ranch in an effort to identify the remains, but nobody recognized the face of the unfortunate, and for some time the group lolled in their saddles and gazed at the deceased, until somebody suggested that the proper thing to do was to send for the coroner at Minnekahta.

Accordingly a messenger was dispatched to the county seat and told the tale to the coroner. Callahan reflected a moment and then asked, "Are you sure he's dead?"

"Awful sure," replied the messenger with conviction.

Callahan reflected again. It was a long, long trail to Horsehead Creek and he was not a strong man.

"Well," he said finally, with official dignity. "be right sure that he's dead, and then bury him deep enough so the coyotes won't get him."

So Fall River County furnishes a precedent for holding coroner's inquests by absent treatment. The vicious element which was fairly numerous among the adventurers who swarmed into the northern Hills at the call of gold, was largely lacking in Fall River county, so there is much less blood and gunpowder in its history than in that of the mining districts. Yet when a community is only half organized and therefore unable to defend itself effectually, there are always men who take advantage of that condition, and lawless individuals— horse thieves, cattle rustlers and others if that ilk were by no means uncommon. A gun was a very familiar instrument to the early citizens, and they did not always carry it because of the abundant wild game of those days.

Martin Valley Ranch, later 7-11 Ranch, is located west of Buffalo Gap and is still a working ranch in 2021.
Photo courtesy Cheryl Martin Zimiga

Among other newcomers of the year 1883, James W. Martin settled on the north edge of the townsite, near where the Wind Cave road now runs. Mr. Martin, who later established the

Eben W. Martin and Norman Mason built the Martin Mason building for their law offices in Deadwood. Martin moved his law practice to Hot Springs in 1909.

Photo courtesy Cheryl Martin Zimiga

Martin Valley ranch, was the father of Eben W. Martin, then a Deadwood attorney, whose name has had so honorable a prominence in Black Hills history from that day to this.

Late that fall E. W. Martin drove down from Deadwood to visit his father, bringing with him his friend, J. L. Denman, also long well-known in the Hills. On the morning after they arrived, all the horses on the place, six head, were missing from the corral and it was suspected that they had been stolen.

Mounts were borrowed from town, but a hunt which lasted two days turned up only two head of the missing stock. On the third night Mr. Martin's mother awakened the men with the whispered announcement that she heard suspicious noises near the corral, and they all sprang up. Mr. Martin was the first to get outdoors, with a double-barreled shotgun in his hands. A few steps from the door, in the gray light of a cloudy moon, he saw a skunk. He really took little stock in the horse thief theory, anyway, and, as he had heard his father complain of the skunks as a nuisance about the place, he promptly raised his gun and let drive at the animal. Immediately another skunk appeared, with skunk-like indifference to danger, and Mr. Martin successfully spent his second barrel upon it. Then he turned back for more shells, just in time to meet Mr. Denman, rushing out of the house with a rifle.

"I've killed two of 'em," announced Mr. Martin, with his mind full of skunks.

"Killed two of 'em!" gasped Mr. Denman, with his mind full of horse thieves. "Good heavens! You're cool about it, Martin, but you're a lawyer and must know what you're doing. Here! I can't see a thing in this light. Take this rifle and go after the rest, and I'll keep you supplied with ammunition."

Then, after a brief explanation, the midnight alarm ended with shouts of laughter which startled the remaining horses in the corral.

Chapter 4
Cowboys and Ladies

The region surrounding Minnekahta, heavily grassed, well watered by the Cheyenne and its tributaries, subject to unusually light snowfall and sufficiently rough to afford livestock abundant shelter, began to attract the attention of open-range cow outfits as early as 1878.

One of the earliest and largest of these was the Bar T outfit on Hat Creek, of which Phil Clark was foreman. Filling the saddles of the Bar T, to quote only a few well-known names, were Henry Marty, Al Powell, Ed Clark and Jim Bell. The TAN ranch, near Oelrichs, later absorbed by the Bar T, had C.B. Green and Charley Roe on its force.

The Bar T Ranch headquarters was located on Hat Creek.
John W.H. Grabill photo, 1890

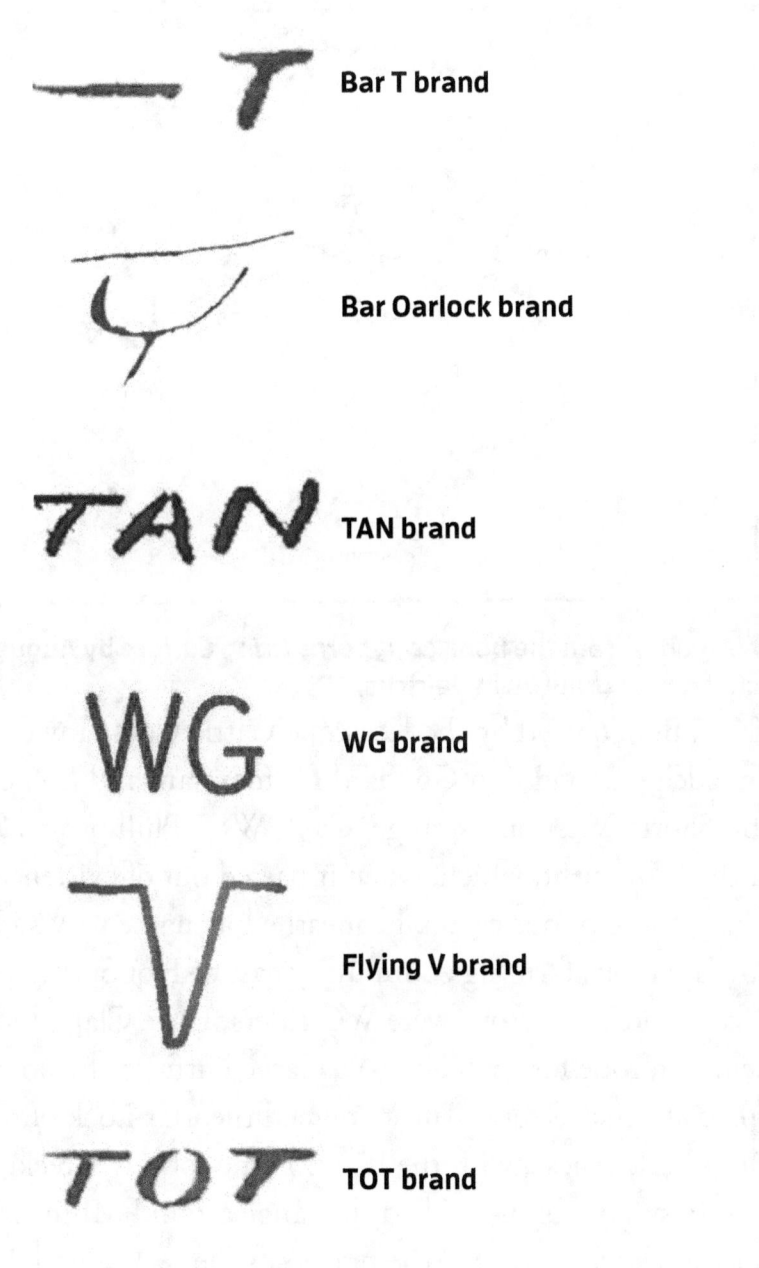

Ranch Brands

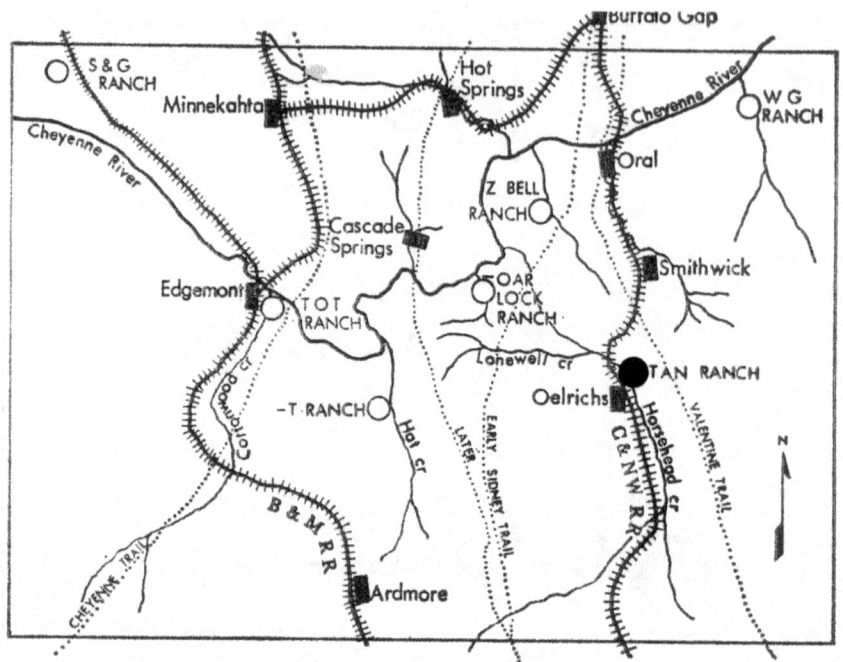

This map is from the book *Longhorns Bring Culture* by August Schatz, who grew up in Oelrichs, SD.

The Z Bell, owned by the Keystone Cattle Company of Philadelphia, had Lon Goddard for foreman, and Louie Green and Shorty West on its range. Capt. W. P. Phillips was foreman of the WG outfit, which, when it passed out of existence after a long and glorious career, bequeathed its name to WG Flat, now a famous farming community east of Hot Springs. Johnny Richer and Ed Parsons were WG riders. Dave Clark and Ed Lemmon rode for the Flying V, a large outfit to the north, on French Creek. George Turner owned the Oar Lock outfit on Dry Creek. These, with the L7 on Lame Johnny Creek, and sundry smaller brands, filled the range around Minnekahta with stock which dotted the prairies, valleys, and park lands, taking the place of the vanished buffalo.

Though never a "cow town" in the dime-novel sense, Minnekahta was located in the heart of a great cow country, and the centaurs of the range played a lively part in the first fifteen years of the town's history. The odd mingling of leather-legged cowhands, blanketed Indians and fashionable eastern health and pleasure- seekers on the streets in the early years struck the note of human variety that has always kept the town from the social dry rot which is the curse of small places with a static population.

A young Indian woman wearing a blanket around her shoulders was camped at Hot Springs.

Horan Collection

Some of the early settlers had never seen a cowboy until they arrived in Minnekahta. Mrs. R. D. Jennings tells amusingly of her first glimpse of them, shortly after she had left the comfort of her old home in "the States" for the little log cabin in the canyon of the warm springs. One morning, while standing at the door of the cabin, her attention was drawn by the thud and scuffle of hoofs at the top of the hill south of the spring, and she saw several horsemen loom above the crest. To her astonishment they turned the noses of their horses down an almost perpendicular footpath on the hillside, and descended as nonchalantly as if riding a level trail. They were wild-looking persons of a sort she had never seen before, and they talked boisterously as they rode.

"By _____! There's a woman," remarked one in a tone of surprise.

"_____ if it ain't," agreed another. "Don't it beat _____ how fast the country's settling up?"

Mrs. Jennings realized that these lurid comments were about her.

Mrs. R. D. (Mattie) Jennings

Alone at the cabin, terrified by the uncouth appearance and brightly tinted language of the strangers, she retreated to her own room, locked the door and tilted a chair against it. Then she peered around the drawn curtains as the horsemen rode in the dooryard. The movies had not yet familiarized the world with the cowpuncher's appearance, and Mrs. Jennings observed with disquiet the wide, floppy hats, the voluminous leather leg garments, ornamented with metal disks, and the spurs of preposterous size on the boot heels. Most alarming of all, however, was the long-barreled revolver slung at each man's hip.

This leather-legged cowhand, Fred Pierce, illustrates how cowboy gear was worn.
John C. H. Grabill photo, 1887

She gazed earnestly at the awful shooting irons and prayed for the return of her husband. Luckily, the besieged lady's prayers were soon answered, and Dr. Jennings came up the trail from the main canyon. To his wife's surprise he greeted the formidable strangers with matter-of-course friendliness and then turned toward the house and called her. She removed the barricading chair, unlocked the door and came out with considerable hesitation. Her fear evaporated, however, as her husband presented the visitors to her and each of the apparent ruffians removed his big hat and acknowledged the introduction, a little awkwardly but with unmistakable courtesy and respect. Mrs. Jennings' fright of the morning ended with a merry dinner in the cabin, where she began a long and cordial acquaintance with the men of the lariat.

The cowboys were popular in town from the first. They liked the town and the town liked them. One reason for their popularity was that they constituted the town's unofficial standing army. The Sioux, though quelled by superior force, were by no means tamed. They were loosely penned on the Reservation, only a few miles away, and at that time—poor wild folks!—they were suffering the restrictions and discomforts of civilization without having learned to enjoy its privileges and pleasures. They had given up the Black Hills with sullen reluctance and the canyon of the springs was the spot in their former domain which they regarded with greatest affection. They still visited the springs, sometimes in numbers which caused uneasiness.

There were troops at Sturgis, on the north and Crawford, Nebraska, on the south, but it was a long, long trail to either post and if the Indians should "get up" in force, they might easily wipe out the handful of white folks at Minnekahta before the unwieldy government could act. Under these conditions the cowpunchers, hardy young men of proven nerve and skilled in the use of firearms, were very comforting persons to have about when Red Cloud and his restive braves were mentioned.

The 13th Cavalry Regiment was organized at Fort Meade, SD

The 3rd Infantry from Fort Robinson near Crawford, was at Hot Springs.

John C. H. Grabill photo

Cowpunchers were ready to defend the community and also enjoyed the social aspects. The octagonal dancing pavilion and the 70-foot bowling alley were constructed in 1889.

"If the Indians break out," the townspeople used to say, "the cowboys won't have to wait for any orders from Washington."

Aside from their role of possible defenders, the cowboys' personal qualities made them favorites in society. The town has always had society with an S, and did even in those sparse and spacious days. The indispensable ingredient in making Society is ladies, and the ladies were here from the first. Often the historian of a western town is compelled to give more or less space in his chronicle to dance-hall girls. In many new western camps most of the feminine element consisted of that unhappy type of womanhood. Fortunately this was not true of Minnekahta. From the thinnest beginnings its social life was as wholesome as that of any older community, and it is proud to remember that its "first ladies" were ladies indeed.

The ladies came over difficult and dangerous ways. Pioneering was rather an enjoyable game to a healthy man, and probably most of the credit for fortitude and heroism should be given to pioneer women. When Mrs. Jennings came up from Sidney, the stage, at one stretch of the journey, made the remarkable speed of forty miles in forty hours. Every few hundred yards during that forty hours, the vehicle would mire in the gumbo and the driver would shout, "All out!" Whereas all the men passengers would descend with muttered profanity and make auxiliary horses of themselves. Mrs. Stewart, likewise, was three days on the road from Deadwood, walking up most of the hills. They were hard roads for ladies to travel, with a hard life at the end of them, yet the ladies came, and stayed.

The late Mrs. F. T. Evans used to tell of a night she spent at Rapid City while on her first trip to Minnekahta.

She was alone in a second-story bedroom of the sketchily-built hotel, and there were wide cracks between the floor boards. In the room below four gentlemen, whose names were afterward widely known in the Hills but will not be given here, had sat for an evening of poker. They had not been playing long when the game reached an exciting turn and Mrs. Evans' ears were assailed by a devastating explosion of pioneer profanity. It was stilled almost immediately, however, by a loud "Sh-h-h!" and the listener in the second story could imagine a masculine finger pointing upward to remind the swearers, not of the wrath of Heaven, but of the near proximity of a shocked and scandalized lady. The game continued decorously for a few minutes, and then—again a crisis, again a blasphemous eruption and again the admonitory "Sh-h-h!" and the uplifted finger. Mrs. Evans was religious and a woman of the truest refinement, but she also possessed a keen sense of humor. The

Mrs. Fred (Theresa M.) Evans
Cross Photo

pathetic efforts of the poor fellows below to bridle their unruly western tongues for her sake amused her so intensely that for an hour she lay wakeful on her lumpy hay tick, shaking with silent laughter every time the gamesters forgot themselves.

Yes; the ladies came early, and the cowboys, in their womanless way of life, appreciated the society which the ladies made. It was said that no flood of the temperamental Cheyenne, in those days, was high enough to keep the Bar T boys and the WG boys from swimming their horses across for a dance in town, but that a rise of three inches in the river was seized upon as an excuse to remain in town for a day or two longer. Dances were the thing. In 1883 a building was erected at what is now the corner of Eighth Street and River Avenue, which became the first saloon on the town site, but before it entered upon its bacchanalian destiny, the shavings were swept off the new pine floor and a dance was held which was one of the outstanding social events of the early days.

The orchestra at these affairs nearly always consisted simply of Matt Bingham and his fiddle. At times Matt was relieved by

Matt Bingham, holding the fiddle, was a popular player for local dances. Bingham was a cowboy and "Zither" Dick (Richard Bassel) was a cook, both on the Bar T ranch.

a cowboy known only by the name of Zither Dick, who was able to extract dance music from that almost forgotten stringed instrument, the zither. These musicians were necessarily not only men of artistic skill, but of great physical endurance, for every dance that was any dance at all lasted until daylight, and some especially successful affairs are spoken of at which *Home Sweet Home* was played at seven o'clock in the morning.

To play a zither, lay the stringed instrument on a table or lap and pluck the strings with a metal pick on the right thumb. The melody is played with the left hand on the fretboard and the right hand accompanies the melody.

In 1884 R. D. Jennings, who was an architect and builder before he became a physician, erected the frame building on Lincoln Avenue which afterward served in turn as the public school and the Catholic church, and is now spending a sturdy and useful old age as the Catholic parish house.

At first, however, it was intended for a community center—though that term had not yet been invented—and was put up by public subscription in which the townsmen and the cowpunchers shared. It was the headquarters of the Minnekahta Literary and Debating Society. In those days the public mind was not crammed and jaded with movies and radio programs, and the people would turn out to listen to a good speech—or even one not so good. In the new hall Judge Dudley, Dr. Stewart, Major Eaton, Dr. Jennings, Mr. LaFleiche and others of oratorical tendencies held forth on

Dr. Jennings designed and built the Lincoln Hall

subjects of public interest, to the instruction and edification of audiences from town and the surrounding ranges.

The hall was also used for roller skating, a sport which was at that time all the rage in the east, and the Minnekahtans devoted themselves to the new accomplishment with the same earnest application which we still give to a new dance or game. It is not likely that the cowboys insisted on skating as they danced—with their spurs on—but it is certain that many a skater seated himself, or herself, with stunning emphasis on the hard pine floor.

And there on many occasions youth and pleasure chased the glowing hours with flying feet, and cowboys of various brands joyously flirted with the town girls in the mellow radiance of kerosene and young romance. The boys were known by their brands. One night a lady who knew little of the cow business asked who one of the young men was. "Oh, that is one of the Bar T boys," was the reply. Shortly afterward she inquired as to the identity of another youth. "One of the Bar T boys," came the answer.

To this lady the syllables, "Bar T" did not suggest the mark on the red hide of a steer, but brought up a dim vision of an elderly foreigner named Barti. So after several more questions about the boys had brought the same reply, she innocently remarked, "What a large family Mr. Barti must have." That is one of the classic jokes of the county.

It is hard for us of today to imagine how men wearing Mexican spurs could dance on a crowded floor with ladies in billowy, toe-length skirts, but many unimpeachable old-timers say it was done. In those days a cowboy was a cowboy, not a movie actor, and generally his wardrobe contained nothing but his professional garb, so at all dances a steady jingle of rowels kept time to Matt Bingham's fiddling.

Probably no Hot Springs maids or matrons will ever be such belles as were those who lived here during the first few years of the town's history. It was a man's country, and the men were mostly single. At every dance or other social function, the men outnumbered the girls at least ten to one, and the competition among the beaux for the smiles of the fair was correspondingly fierce. It speaks well for the diplomacy and good sense of the pioneer girls that the early annals are not marred with many murders.

Claude Tillotson was a cowboy ready to dance, spurs and all

Socially the young men of less romantic callings were at a sad disadvantage compared to the cowboys. They could not come dashing over the horizon to dances on snorting broncs. They had no flaming neckerchiefs, no chaps, no spurs, no six-shooters.

They were not in the least picturesque in their badly wrinkled suits of citizen's clothes, so generally the girls danced with the bespurred buckaroos, and the less decorative males spent most of the evening standing in corners, covertly sneering at the frank swaggers of the cowpunchers.

At one time, when the young men of the town had grown sufficiently numerous to rebel against the cowpuncher monopoly, they organized a dance which was an invitation affair and took great care that no news of it should get out among the ranches. But inevitably a girl who liked cowboys—and what girl didn't?—betrayed the secret and the word flew across the range almost as swiftly as a radio wave travels nowadays. Every ranch within reasonable—or unreasonable—distance declared a holiday and turned out in force, even to the horse-wrangler and the cook. On the appointed day, according to the account of an old-time girl, it looked during the late afternoon, as if were being attacked by a regiment of cavalry.

Along every trail pillars of dust arose into the sky, and soon troops of riders descended upon the startled town with thundering hoofs and joyous yells. Invitation or no invitation, there was no excluding them from the dance, so in the hall of the Literary and Debating Society there was a sound of revelry by night, accompanied by far more than the customary jingling of spurs. At five o'clock the next morning the exhausted but still laughing ladies declared the ball a great success, though the town youths, who had spent most of the night in corners as usual, said things of another sort under their breath.

Perhaps we harp too much on the hardships of the pioneers. True, they lacked some conveniences and luxuries, yet the stories of those days from the people who were a part of them are full of abounding high spirits. Apparently the old-timers whined less over their undoubted hardships than we do over slight discomforts, while they took their simple pleasures with a wholehearted enjoyment which our more sophisticated and self-conscious generation would be almost ashamed to show. Ladies and cowboys! The ladies we still have with us, some of the older generation, some of the new, and all charming, as they ever were and ever will be. But the boys—ah, the cowboys! We still have elderly veterans whose eyes gleam when they speak of the good old days on the range, but they are "gentled" out of all semblance of their old-time engaging cussedness.

Ward Stanley on the left and George Marty were two of the old-time cowboys who rode the open range in Fall River and adjoining counties.

We still have athletic young men who wear big hats and high-heeled boots, and know the look of a steer and the feel of a horse. But the dear old open-range cowboy has forever ridden over the skyline into the sunset, and pulled off his creaky saddle on the far slope of the Last Divide.

Supper at open range roundup camp on Cheyenne River at mouth of Plum Creek, June 23, 1903. An enlarged photo complete with identification is located at the Pioneer Museum, Hot Springs, SD.

Chapter 5
The Pup Gets Its Eyes Opened

Minnekahta was now about five years old. Its growth had not been swift enough to make any fortunes in real estate. In fact, after five years, an observer on the brow of College Hill might be able to count thirteen buildings, including barns. And most of these buildings were of logs. The town had never been bothered with any ambition to become a commercial center, but sometimes Stewart and Jennings, gazing upon the empty canyon, would loose their imagination and indulge the fancy that some day it might contain a health resort of two or three thousand people, while their wives, with the sturdy conservatism of women, would laugh at their dreams.

But dreams sometimes come true if the dreamers are constant enough, and in the year 1885 an event occurred thirteen miles away, which tended to revive any flagging faith in the town's future. The North Western, or rather the Fremont, Elkhorn and Missouri Valley, reached Buffalo Gap on its way to Deadwood.

There was a great tooting of locomotives and clanking of steel and swearing of gang bosses at the Gap, and that hamlet suddenly became very ambitious and rather sinful. By night the smoky air of saloons was full of the clink of glass and the whirr of the "wheel" and the slap of cards and the noisy and highly improper conversation of the bunch that always followed a new railroad in those days. By day the ancient and dishonorable game of the three shells claimed its victims on the open street. The town enjoyed a period of feverish prosperity. Great stretches of buffalo grass on all sides were laid out in sudden gridirons of town lots, for the Gap also had its dreamers. Those dreams never came true in their entirety, but the Gap is still a good town—much more "good" now than in those days, from all accounts and the future is still a wide, wide country.

Blacksmith W.T. Grubbs did a booming business in Buffalo Gap.

All this stirred Minnekahta very deeply. It meant that the distance from the railroad was shortened from nearly two hundred miles to thirteen. It meant that if the town bestirred itself a little the railroad would actually come into the canyon some day, and stage travel would be a thing of the past. The whole population, at various times took opportunities to drive over to the Gap and look at the sinful but stirring main street. Then they would gaze with interest at a snorting locomotive—some of them for the first time in years—and come back to their quiet canyon full of optimism for the future. The town had laughed and danced its way through its childish years, but now it began to yearn to grow up. It was at about this time that Dr. Stewart cut his homestead on College Hill into town lots, and offered them at very liberal terms, to wit, he would make a present of a lot to anybody who would build on it. In the early days the only way to drive from the upper to the lower town was to go over the hill and through what is now the Sanitarium orchard, but a road down the canyon—the forerunner of River Avenue—had been opened. The work had been done by "all hands and the cook," even the children cutting brush and carrying rocks. What is now lower Minnekahta Avenue was still a problem, being a spongy bog which, as the old-timers say, "not even a cat could cross."

Occasionally somebody's cow would get mired there, and would have to be roped and dragged out at the end of a lariat.

Christmas night of 1885 saw a particularly big dance at the hall of the Literary and Debating Society, but during the afternoon of the same day a more important event took place there, when Eva Jackson and John G. Richer were united in marriage. It was as near a formal affair as was possible in those days, and many guests were present. Ed Lemmon, a Flying V boy, and his sweetheart acted as best man and bridesmaid. The bridegroom seemed to have taken the affair very coolly but the best man suffered from stage fright. Ed would have been quite at home in the noise and confusion of a roundup, or even a dance, but the deadly formal silence of the assembled company, as the bridal party walked up the aisle, swamped him in a sudden wave of terror. As the four reached the dais and faced the justice of the peace, Ed saw the back door ahead of him and made for it. He said afterward that he didn't intend to stop short of the top of Battle Mountain. But alas! the door was locked. The unhappy best man turned slowly on his high bootheel, while the guests struggled to maintain their gravity, and wandered uncertainly back to stand in his proper place as Justice of the Peace LaFleiche pronounced the fateful words. For everyone but Ed, however, the wedding was a happy affair and, like most of the pioneer weddings, the beginning of a true partnership which only death could break.

The unholy influence of that wicked neighbor, Buffalo Gap, made itself felt in Minnekahta on New Year's Eve, 1885. On the word of an old-time belle, every man in town was in a state of alcoholic exaltation that night, except two young fellows who had thoughtlessly agreed to make a watch party with their lady friends and see the old year out. These uneasy gallants forgot to talk to the girls, as they listened wistfully to the shooting and shouting at the saloon, and watched the clock, waiting for it to strike twelve so they could join the riot.

The year 1886 was eventful, one of the high spots in the town's history. It had been hopeless to do much toward building a city 200 miles from the railroad, but 13 miles was only a step, even in those days of slow horseflesh. The company, originally formed in 1882, was now reorganized, and as the Dakota Hot Springs Company played a leading part in the town's history for a number of years afterward. Mr. F. T. (Fred) Evans was president; Hon. E. G. (Judge) Dudley, vice-president; Dr. R. D. Jennings, secretary; Mr. L. R. Graves of Deadwood, treasurer, and Dr. A. S. Stewart, superintendent.

These officials and their associates were a notable group of pioneers, and no town can trace its beginnings to men who averaged higher in intelligence, energy and character. Headed by Fred Evans, a bearded giant of a man who had made a fortune in various sorts of transportation, ranging from street cars in Sioux City to "bull" freight outfits between Pierre and Deadwood, they went confidently to work to make a city of a score of ramshackle log buildings, located in a lonely canyon 13 miles from a branch railroad.

The bull team was widely used by freighters such as Fred Evans.

They were splendid gamblers, more daring than any man who ever played the wheel or bucked faro, for they were backing their bets, not with a handful of greenbacks or a sack of yellow dust, but with their whole futures. And the game involved more than their money. Their hearts were in it. A man loves the town where he was born with the same quiet, matter-of-course affection that he gives his mother, but those founders and builders, gathered from many home towns, seemed to have loved their new city with something of the passionate, possessive ardor that a man feels toward his sweetheart. This is shown by their subsequent history.

Though they were genuine westerners—adventurous, born with the itching foot and the eye that always sees greener pastures farther on—and though they were men of ability, capable of making their way anywhere, nearly all of the pioneers stuck to the town without wavering, through later years of the blackest discouragement.

Not one of them got rich. Most of them, first and last, "quit lower," but they stayed. This sketch has no room for biography, but one point in the life-histories of the officials of the company of 1886 is worth noting. L. R. Graves, of course, was a Deadwood man, but all the rest—Evans, Dudley, Jennings and Stewart—lived out their lives in the canyon, died here, and their mortal dust lies forever under its red soil. Similar statements would be true of Turner, Trimmer, the Pettys and nearly all of the substantial old- timers. Loyalty to one's home town is everywhere stressed at present, but as a rule that loyalty lasts only so long as it is profitable. All through the history of Hot Springs, however, there have been people who stayed in it at little profit to themselves—sometimes at a distinct loss—and there have been many who went away and came back.

All that the townsmen of today say in praise of Hot Springs is not mere "boosting." There is a charm about the place. Those who know it best will confess that it is no Golconda, no El Dorado, but—"You'll like Hot Springs"—that is a true and time-tried slogan.

During 1886, among other changes, "Hot Springs" became officially and permanently the name of the town. There has been considerable fault found with the name, and with justice. For one thing it is inaccurate, for the springs are not hot. For another, with many similarly named places in the country, it is confusing. Shortly after the railroad came and the name was changed, Mrs. A. S. Stewart, thinking to take advantage of the new and swift means of communications, sent to Chicago to get a pretty dress for her daughter Blanche, now Mrs. W. H. Stanley, who was then a scrap of a girl. Blanche waited, but the dress came not. As was found out afterward, it first meandered down to Hot Springs, Arkansas; then back to Chicago, and then to various other places before it finally made its way to its proper destination, arriving after the better part of a year of travel. It was a pretty dress, but by the time it came the girl had actually outgrown it. Similar things happen yet.

"Wi-wi-la-kahta" might have been too cumbrously poetical for Anglo-Saxon tongues, but "Minnekahta" or "Minnekahta Springs" would have been distinctive, pretty and a lasting memorial to our fellow-townsmen, the Sioux. However, at the time the place was named, Hot Springs, Arkansas, Hot Sulphur Springs, Virginia, and such results were already famous, and probably the name was taken as a quick and inexpensive way of advertising the town as a watering place. Once it is fixed, a poor name, like a poor reputation, is a hard thing to shake off, so Hot Springs, like the beloved but poorly named Black Hills, will probably keep its present appellation until the end of time.

Today there are few small towns that have as many fine

buildings to be proud of as has Hot Springs, and the first pretentious building on the site was erected in the epochal year of 1886. It was called the Minnekahta Hotel, and was built by the company on the present site of the Evans.

The Minnekahta Hotel and the Petty Livery Barn in the distance show the narrow canyon.
Arundel C. Hull, Eugene Arundel Collection

One hundred and fifty thousand feet of native Black Hills pine went into its construction, while the flooring and finishing lumber came over the new railroad to the Gap from the east. R. D. Jennings designed it and it was a three-story structure, 40 by 128, with a two-story wing at the rear, which covered 60 by 30 feet.

It was provided with steam heat and hot and cold water and, as will be seen, was a tremendous leap from the era of log cabins. The rates, as recorded, were from $6.00 to $21.00 per week, and the advertising promised "all the delicacies of the season."

This undated photo shows the first Hot Springs Star office in Hot Springs.

Another notable event of 1886 was the establishment of the town's first newspaper, The *Star*, by Dr. Stewart and Mr. W. W. LaFleiche.

It was then printed in a small building near what is now the corner of Seventh Street and River Avenue. The *Star* has changed management several times since then, but it continues to shine upon the town with undimmed luster.

Of interest in this connection was the publication, in the same year, of the first advertising booklet Hot Springs ever put out, the ancestor of many subsequent bits of literature by which the citizens have "tried to tell the world." John Richer has one copy of this booklet, which he has religiously preserved through forty years, and a few quotations from it are irresistible.

> # HOT SPRINGS STAR.
> ### BENEDICT & HANFORD,
> #### PROPRIETORS.
>
> ## FRIDAY, JANUARY 15, 1892.
>
> Published every Friday, at $2.50 per Year.
> Three months......75c | Six months.........$1.25
> Terms invariably in advance.
>
> ### F. F. & M. V. TIME TABLE.
>
> BLACK HILLS PASSENGER.
> Leaves Hot Springs...................3:45 a. m
> Arrives   "   "   ....9:15 p. m
> CHICAGO EXPRESS.
> Leaves Hot Springs ....7:35 p. m.
> Arrives "   "   ....5:35 a. m.
> Freight leaves at.....................10:00 a. m.
>   "   arrives at.....................1:30 p. m
>
> A. D. WOOD, Agent.
>
> ### B & M R R TIME TABLE.
>
> East, departs ....5:40 p. m.
> West,   "   ....7:00 a. m.
> East, arrives........................8:20 a. m.
> West   "   ....7:00 p. m.
> Tickets on sale for all points east, west, north and south.   H. T. CATLIN, Agent.

It begins its description of the town, as it then stood, with the following quatrain:

> "Our Union is springs, mountain, river and sky;
>
> Man breaks not the medal when God cuts the die!
>
> Though racked is the frame with agonies real,
>
> No case is so bad but the waters will heal."

From a purely literary standpoint this poem leaves something to be desired, but it has the advantage over some of the greatest poems in the language of containing much sober truth.

The booklet is illustrated with several old-fashioned cuts. One shows the present Minnekahta Avenue, with the Jennings log cabin and the bath house (about the size of a one-car garage) in the foreground, and the new Minnekahta Hotel at the mouth

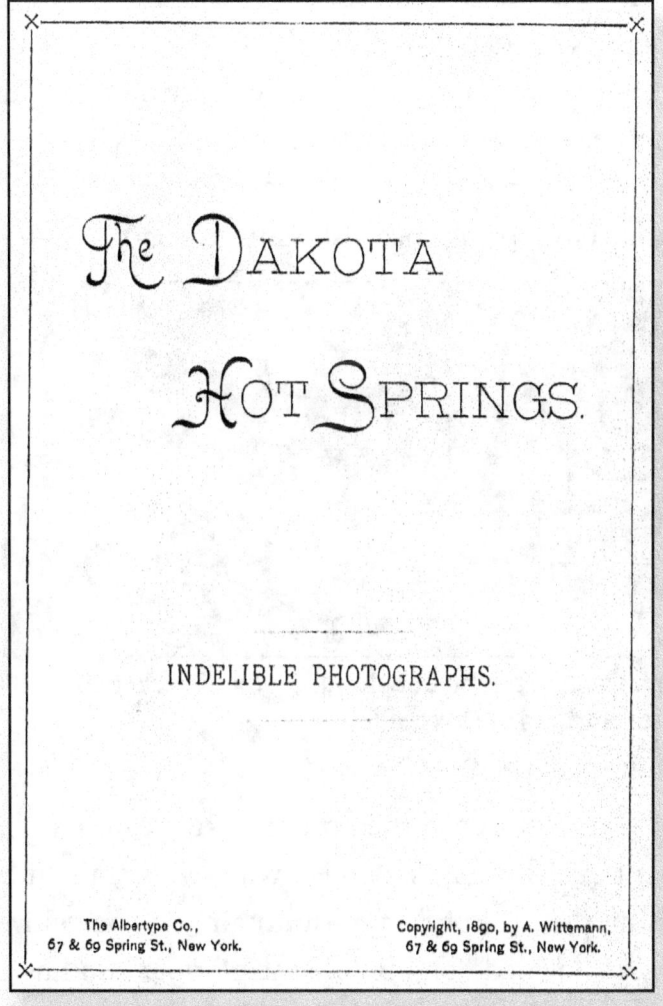

of the gulch in the background. Another sketch, taken from the present site of the Braun, shows the old Iowa House, and, beyond, the Minnekahta—and that's all. The new Minnekahta was played up for all it was worth in the illustrations, as in the text.

For a resort town, the place takes a high moral tone. Hear this: "The company is determined to keep all objectionable characters from the vicinity of the springs and from town. No gambling games or devices will be allowed, and the hard and disreputable class which invariably follows such institutions will be persistently tabooed." Take that, Buffalo Gap, Deadwood and the rest of you! Neither a Roaring Camp nor a Monte Carlo, Hot Springs has always been good.

The caption reads: "Tallyho Coaching. Sioux City party Coaching at the Great Hot Springs of Dakota."
John C. H. Grabill photo 1889

Here's the way you reached the Springs forty years ago: "Magnificent tally-ho stages connect with every train at Buffalo Gap, reaching the base of Battle Mountain, just beyond which the Springs are located, long before the glorious sun has gone to its crimson couch in the far-distant Occident."

Here's what you do after you get there: "The absence of fashionable amusements and dissipation all facilitate a rapid cure and complete restoration to health. But the visitor is never at a loss for amusement, and every day spent in this fairyland is a succession of surprises. The hotel is only a few yards from the banks of the Falling Water River, where the water goes merrily

The warm water-based health spa businesses in Hot Springs have been a draw and continue to be so in 2021. The Evans Hotel, on the right, was touted as the finest hotel between Chicago and Denver, at the time. Now called the Evans, it is an apartment building. The photo caption attached reads: "Arrival via the Fremont, Elkhorn & Missouri Valley R.R. of the first section of the National Association of Railway Surgeons at Hot Springs in the Black Hills, S. Dak. June 6th, '93, showing The Evans and Gillespie Hotels."
W. R. Cross photo

babbling, bubbling, purling, gurgling, swiftly flowing on."

"Falling Water River"—did you get that? Too bad that name couldn't have been retained. "Fall River" is borrowed from a New England manufacturing town, a place of noise and crowds and narrow sky lines, and doesn't fit the little stream nearly so well as "Falling Water."

But the poetry of the whole booklet! Innumerable descriptions of Hot Springs and the Black Hills have been written since the day of this early scribe, but no matter how coolly statistical and conscientiously accurate the writer is at the beginning of his article, he invariably strews armfuls of poetical flowers in the pathway of his readers before he finishes. The roughest and rockiest soil of the region seems to sprout poetry as freely as it sprouts pine trees, and no visiting writer has ever been able to escape the lyrical infection.

In this same interesting year of 1886, a writer for the *Commercial Gazette* of Cincinnati, sends his paper a very sober travelogue concerning his journey through northern Nebraska, and even holds his pen down to prosaic language during his passage of the Bad Lands. Then he crosses the Cheyenne and approaches Hot Springs, and lo! he smites his lyre and sings:

> "Crossing the Cheyenne River we feel the wonderful exhilaration of going 'On and up where Nature's heart
> Beats strong among the hills.'
> The meadows roll and swell in billowy waves, bearing like white, speckled foam upon their crests a sea of
> daisies, with here and there a patch of crimson clover or a golden haze of buttercups."

A representative of the *Daily Journal*, of Kansas City, visiting Hot Springs in the same year, undertakes to give his readers an account of the therapeutic value of the springs, and does so with more or less calmness. But the "healing waters" seem to have an intoxicating effect, and soon he bursts out: "Here the undisguised face of nature presents itself with wonderful effect—hillside and bank of stream, whispering trees and clinging moss, glistering waterfall and fragrant flowers, walls of rock and quiet glens, the harmonies of sunlight and foliage, clouds and mountain peaks, frowning chasms and wide-stretching landscapes!"

Of course all this was back in the bad old days of abundant alcohol, yet the same sort of language was indulged in at that time by visiting members of the clergy, and even since prohibition writing men of all classes wield singing pens whenever they try to give topographical data about Hot Springs. It must be the nature of the place—now, as forty years ago—and so long as the clear little river "goes merrily babbling, bubbling, purling, gurgling, swiftly flowing on," the canyon of Wi-wi-la-kahta will inspire colorful verbiage.

Chapter 6
Religion, Law and Literature

As a pleasure resort, one would naturally expect Hot Springs to be a worldly place, and it may be that a trifle of worldliness has been discernable in the canyon at times. But the pioneers were almost without exception people of old American stock—look over their names—and that assured the town a rock bottom of religious conviction which showed just as soon as the cloudy waters of the early community life began to clear.

The Chautauqua grounds, located on the northern edge of Hot Springs, was the setting for a 1914 Protestant church service. In 2021, the spot is still known as Chautauqua Park.

As far back as 1884 the Protestant women began to yearn for the familiar religious activities they had known in their various churches "back home," and organized an aid society. The society enrolled itself under the standard of the Methodist church, not because the ladies were all Methodists, but because the preachers of that large denomination seemed more numerous out in the wilds of the new country than other clergymen, and could more frequently be obtained to hold services.

As all the houses in town were small, these occasional Protestant services were held in the open air whenever possible.

The sandstone Catholic Church was constructed next to the Lincoln Hall.

One can imagine that on those still, brilliant mornings so frequent in the Hot Springs climate, the voice of prayer floating over the bowed heads of the congregation and up toward the incredible blue of the Black Hills sky would be as impressive of any cathedral service.

The sheep of the Catholic flock who had wandered into

this remote canyon were first gathered under one of their shepherds one morning in 1887, at a service in a building which stood opposite the present site of the court house. Like the Protestants, they had no regular place of worship for some time, but finally bought the building on Lincoln Avenue which had been used as a skating rink and public school. This they remodeled into adequate quarters for that day, and since then the parish has had a record of steady progress, culminating in the erection of their handsome stone church in 1926.

In the year of the first Catholic service, 1887, the combined Protestant group had grown strong enough to build a Methodist church, which still stands.

The first Methodist church built in Hot Springs

Later, as the population increased, members of the various Protestant persuasions grew numerous enough to have their own places of worship and their own clergy. Hot Springs has always been very well churched. Probably there are few small towns in which so many shades of religious thought have established more or less permanent organizations as in Hot Springs during the last forty years. In most respects the town bears little resemblance to Athens, but in considering the number of its sects, past and present, one is likely to think of a sentence in Saint Paul's famous sermon to the Athenian philosophers on Mars Hill. (How many church members get that without looking it up? Please don't all speak at once.) Yet in its business of curing the ills of the flesh and catering to seekers of pleasure, no doubt Hot Springs needs all the religion available. Under whatever name or creed, the church is the organized conscience of the community, and the community would be in sorry plight without it.

Reference has been made to the pious resolution of the company of 1886 in regard to gambling. For the most part it was lived up to, which is a tremendous statement when one considers the influential position occupied by the old-time western professional gambler in most of the Hills towns at the time.

As to alcohol, however, intoxicating liquors played too large a part in the life of the day for anybody to think of excluding them, especially from a resort town. The first saloon, as has been mentioned, went up in 1883, and was followed by others as the number of inhabitants and thirsts increased.

The saloon of the Old West was often more or less of a social center for men, rather than merely a center of dissipation. Old-timers remember it as a conference room, a debating hall and a sort of luncheon club. It was the usual rendezvous of townsmen and ranchmen to discuss business matters and frequently the

The Eureka is on the far right. The August 12, 1904 Hot Springs Star said that John G. Stetter was the proprietor of the Eureka, one of the foremost drinking resorts in the "Vale of Minnekahta".

drinking was quite incidental. For many years a good part of the male population of Hot Springs thus made use of such places as "The Eureka" and "The Bodega" of pungent memory.

The temperance element in the town was always strong and active, however. During periods when even the teetotalers among the men were indifferent on the subject, groups of determined women kept up the fight for the curtailing or abolition of the liquor traffic. In the end, partly because of their propaganda and partly because of changing conditions which minimized the slight good of the saloon and glaringly emphasized its evils, the day came when the Hot Springs barkeeper swabbed his mahogany for the last time. As a matter

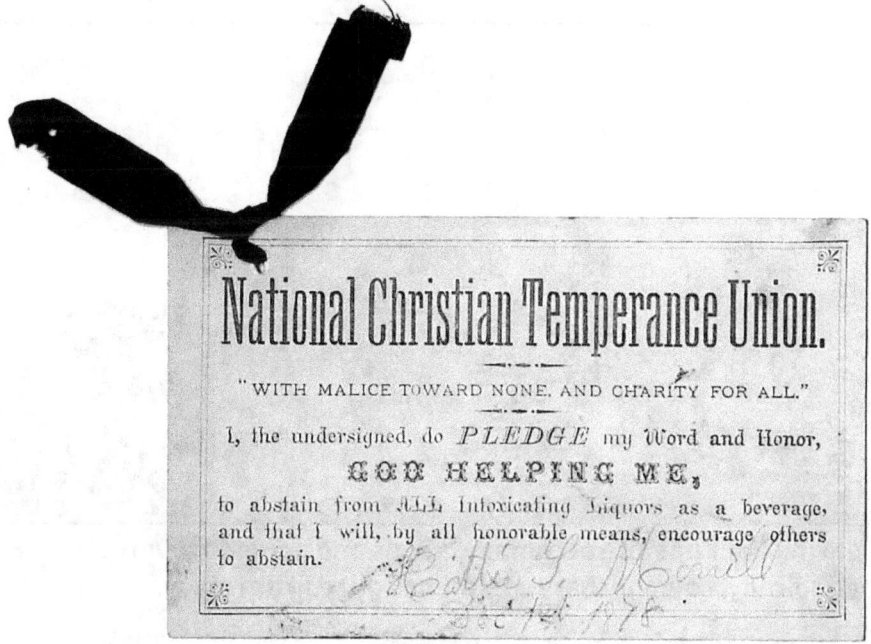

of recent history, Hot Springs maintained its reputation for progressiveness by "going dry" before either the state or the nation took that step.

But the rough work of pioneering made equally rough play inevitable, and the penetrating odor of whiskey will always linger about the early annals of Western towns. The life of that day, while it looks interesting to us who think only of its more exciting episodes, was in the main monotonous. In the loneliness, the isolation and lack of the spice of life, the women as they always do, just did the best they could and behaved themselves, but men were sorely tempted to find surcease from dullness in artificial excitement. This was especially true of the cowboys, who often came to town wild to get the dust of the range out of their throats and the eternal bawling of cattle out of their ears.

Leaving their pasture accommodations and going to town periodically, cowpunchers sometimes got a little rowdy.

This they accomplished rather recklessly, expressing their signs of relief through the muzzles of their six-shooters, but the fact that these little celebrations had no result beyond some harmless noise shows the absence of vicious intent. In Hot Springs on several occasions, some exuberant cowboy staged the traditional cow-country stunt of riding his horse into the saloon and shooting out the lights, while unmounted customers dived behind the bar or went through the windows "all spraddled out" but nobody was hurt and the property damage was paid for.

There is a groggy old Hot Springs story which has to do with two citizens, nameless here, going down the canyon and across the creek, one evening, to call on a third citizen, whom we will leave equally anonymous. The host had a private keg of chokecherry wine, known then as "cherry bounce," and his wife was absent, so a pleasant evening was enjoyed by all.

Toward midnight the two guests, not drunk, but wobbling somewhat both intellectually and physically, started for home. There was not a wagon bridge in the town—nor the county—at that time, and the two unsteady pedestrians, missing the log footbridge at the ford, struck into the river and waded up the bed of the stream.

"Gosh!" remarked one, as he splashed along. "Stars are out, but there must 'a been a big shower while we were in the house."

"Shower!" rejoined the other. "This was a cloudburst. Never seen so much water runnin' down this road before."

After a hundred feet of slipping on stones and struggling against the swift current the pilgrims were weary and one sat down on a submerged boulder in midstream, while the other sank to his knees beside his friend and they steadied each other with a mutual embrace.

"Say, I got an idea," said one a few minutes later. "Listen, this water's warm. This ain't the road at all. It's the creek."

The other man solemnly dipped an experimental hand into the water which already immersed him to his shoulder blades.

"Ol' man, I b'lieve you're right," he said. "You're a great thinker. But you got one fault that will keep you from ever bein' a great man—you're too darn slow about reachin' a conclusion."

Fall River runs through the center of Hot Springs. The river's warm water never freezes.

There is another old story about the creek—nonalcoholic this time—which shows that the thermal waters of the stream have other uses besides the healing of disease.

The Fall River road used to cross the creek fourteen times between town and the Falls. One winter day in '85 or thereabouts Bill Wyatt was riding his pony up the canyon and idly watching a load of hay which was bumping along ahead, with the driver walking alongside.

As the weather was bitterly cold, Wyatt thought nothing of the teamster making his way afoot, but when the wagon came to one of the numerous fords the cowboy stiffened in his saddle with astonishment to see the man stop his horses and then deliberately drop into one of the pools and sit there with the water above his waist. He got up directly and, while the sharp wind stiffened his soaked clothing, urged the slow team onward. In a few minutes the wagon reached another ford, and again the driver immersed himself. By this time, Wyatt, bursting with curiosity, came loping up and recognized the eccentric teamster as Joe Marty.

"Joe," he cried. "You drunk?"

"Drunk nothing!" retorted Marty, sitting in the water as contentedly as the historic squaw. "When I forded the Cheyenne an hour ago I had some trouble with my horses and fell in the river. I was as cold as a dead well-digger in no time, and if I hadn't met up with this blessed creek I'd have been froze to death and laid out alongside the road as stiff as a poker by now."

So far as can be learned, the first regular session of circuit court was held in Hot Springs in 1888. The one-story frame building still in use at the corner of Seventh Street and Chicago Avenue was then used as a court house.

The county, while sometimes a trifle noisy, was generally peaceful, and up to that time serious conflicts of interest between citizens had been disposed of before the justice of the peace, thrashed out in court elsewhere, settled with fists or in very rare instances, with six-shooters.

Yet contention existed here, as it always does among humans, and on that morning in 1888 the citizenry took a long step forward in civilization. Thereafter, instead of adjusting their differences with sweeping vituperation and physical violence, they adopted the policy of sitting quietly at the counsel table while their attorneys, under the eye of His Honor, contended fiercely for them with the amazing thrust and parry of legal swordplay—and later told each other funny stories in the street outside. It is an index of the county's general mildness, even in the old days, that this first case was not a murder, but a prosaic lawsuit involving a sum of money.

Court procedure was slightly rough and ready at the beginning, as was natural. There is a tale of a litigant who enticed an opposition witness into a strong room and locked him up there just before he was called to the stand, but that may be an exaggeration. Also a story is told of a cowman on the witness stand who reached back toward his hip with the innocent intention of stimulating his mental processes with a chew of tobacco. The lawyer on the other side, misreading the witness's motion, instantly whipped out a six-shooter and covered him, saying, "Not much! You don't get the drop on me." The witness, however, calmly extricated a rectangular slab of a plug from his pocket, bit a "horseshoe" out of it and, stowing the refreshment in his cheek, regarded the peppery lawyer with a bland, lopsided smile. This latter incident was during the trial of ten of the "Shirt Tail Canyon bunch" for alleged illegal butchering of cattle, which resulted in acquittal.

Since those days the legal profession has always been most ably represented in Hot Springs. It is interesting to note that the

Joe Marty and his brother Henry came to the Black Hills along with C.V. Gardner's bull train in 1876. The brothers started cowboying at the Bar T ranch in 1878. When Fall River County held their first election, Joe was elected sheriff; he served from 1884 to 1887. Joe bought and ran the Bar Oarlock ranch which he sold to his cattle partner, William F. Wyatt, in 1902.

Photo courtesy of Stu Marty

present State's Attorney, Dean Eastman, and his immediate predecessor in that office, Clifford Wilson, are both sons of pioneer Hot Springs lawyers. The late S. E. Wilson, besides serving as the town's first superintendent of schools, had a long and distinguished career as a lawyer while C. S. Eastman, an equally well-known pioneer, is still in active practice.

W. B. ("Bill") Dudley, besides other claims to distinction, holds the record among the profession for length of residence.

S.E. (Stephen Eugene) Wilson and daughter Edith were seated in his law office which was located in the Fall River County courthouse.

His father, Hon. E. O. Dudley, lawyer and vice-president of the Company, was one of the earliest and most prominent of the Hot Springs pioneers, and way back in '88 Bill and his late brother, Jay, were wrangling their father's horses on the slopes of Battle Mountain.

Every town now and then entertains an angel unawares, and probably the first unrecognized angel in Hot Springs was Kennett Harris. Mr. Harris is now one of the best-known writers of Western fiction in the magazine world, but when he showed up here in the eighties he was just a somewhat wistful young Englishman who was trying to find his place in the world. His quest in this vicinity lasted several years, during which he was the county's first clerk of courts, a newspaper editor and even the publisher of a magazine, but to the last he apparently failed to find what he wanted. The failure was only apparent, however, for he really struck the end of the rainbow right in Hot Springs in the form of literary raw material which, since worked up into finished goods with rare skill, has made him famous.

"Ken" as the old-timers speak of him, had strong literary aspirations even in those days. The town had a good journalistic mouthpiece after 1886 in the *Star*, and two years later the *Herald* commenced publication, but the older inhabitants will never forget *The Hatchet*, which was published by Harris in collaboration with C. T. ("Chet") Martin, now editor of the *Valley Irrigator*, at Newell.

The Hatchet was edited somewhat on the order of its Wyoming contemporary, Bill Nye's *Laramie Boomerang*. It was witty, and quotations from it still turn up on conversation among old residents.

For instance, the divided skirt was just coming into use for horseback riding among Western women, as the roughness of the trail made the old sidesaddle dangerous. It was a floppy, awkward garment, with which few women of this

Both legs were on the same side of the horse when riding sidesaddle. Riding sidesaddle was considered more proper for a lady than riding astride.

Photo courtesy Dawn Stevens

free age would cumber themselves, but in that primmer day it was regarded as being brazenly immodest. Harris, as an Englishman, naturally sided with the conservative. "When a skirt is divided against itself," he wrote, "its name is Pants." Many such quips made *The Hatchet* a literary success, but Ken, like most literary men, seemed to lack business acumen, and financially the paper was a failure. He also started a monthly magazine called The Hesperian, which met a similar fate.

In fact, he suffered the slings and arrows of outrageous fortune while in Hot Springs, in a way which is fully up to the traditions of a great literary man's youthful struggles.

On the other hand he had preserved from happier days a full

outfit of evening clothes. He hesitated to wear this costume to dances at first, fearing some jocose violence on the part of the cowpunchers, but finally put it on and, in the phrase of today, got away with it. It was the only suit of its kind in the county at that time, and was regarded with approval by his fellow-townsmen, as being a symbol of local progress in culture. Even the cowboys, suspicious and inclined to be derisive at first, finally came to look upon Ken Harris' "Bald faced shirt and clawhammer coat" as something to be pointed out to strangers with pride.

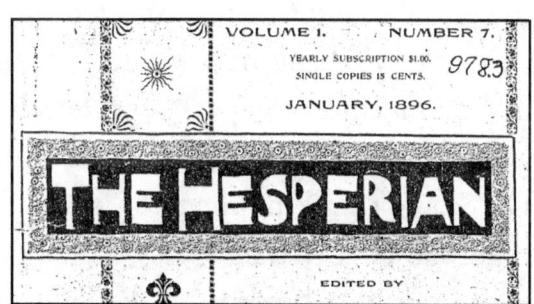

Once during his earlier Hot Springs days he volunteered to guide a party to Wind Cave, which was then little known to the townspeople. The party, besides Harris, consisted of Mrs. A.S. Stewart and her daughter Blanche, Elizabeth Berrier (afterwards Mrs. Jay Crane), Ed Colwell and the two Stewart boys, Harry and Charles. They started at three o'clock in the morning, to be sure of ample time in which to make the trip. Just where they went during that day none of them can tell. A certain poet once wrote that he loved "the little roads to God Knows Where," and Harris, being a literary man, may have had similar tastes. Under his guidance it took the pilgrims from three o'clock in the morning until seven at night to reach the Cave—less than twelve miles as the crow flies. Arrived there, the girls, Harris and Colwell, as the custom then was, tied the end of a ball of string to a tree and entered the Cave, unwinding the string as they went, and leaving Mrs. Stewart and the boys outside. Here Harris again distinguished himself by losing track of the clue and keeping his charges in the gloomy caverns so long that, when they came out, Mrs. Stewart was in tears and Charley, naughtily impatient, was threatening to cut the string which connected the explorers with the upper air and leave them to their fate. By some fortunate combination of circumstances the party covered the distance home in fairly good time, and arrived at four o'clock in the morning to find Dr. Stewart walking the floor in sleepless anxiety nursing a nightmarish idea that a stray bunch of renegade Indians had wiped out his whole family. Perhaps twenty-five hours for a trip to the Cave and back stands as a record, and it was generally agreed among his friends that, as a guide, Ken Harris was an able writer.

It is many years since Mr. Harris has been in the canyon. No doubt he knows more about New York, London and Paris than about the Hot Springs of today. Yet it is clear that he has not forgotten his days beside the warm creek, for in nearly every story he writes, as a regular contributor to that great publication which has the largest circulation in the world, the background of the action is unmistakably the little old Hot Springs that he knew, and he often christens his fiction characters with the names of men who still do business upon River Avenue.

In his daily walk and conversation, Kennett Harris has become a citizen of the world, but in his memory and affections he is yet a citizen of Hot Springs.

Chapter Seven
Boom!

In 1889 the Territory of Dakota, like the life-cell that scientists tell us about, entered upon a new stage of growth by splitting itself in two, and became the states of North and South Dakota. Both states got a thrill out of this comparable to the exultation of a boy in his first long trousers, but that year is probably more memorable to Hot Springs than to any other town in the twin Dakotas.

By this time the Burlington and Elkhorn Railroads, on their lines to the northern Hills, lay west and east of town so close that the smoke of their passing trains could be seen from the top of Battle Mountain. Moreover, it was practically assured that they would build into the canyon of the warm springs at an early date. In those days of traveling from four to six miles an hour—when weather and roads would permit traveling at all—the coming of the railroad to town meant far more than it does now. The citizens had grown accustomed to the daily arrival of the "magnificent tally-ho coaches" from Buffalo Gap, and now Pettys had established a stage line to the nearest station on the new Burlington, but the idea of the actual puff and clang of locomotives right in the quiet little canyon stimulated everybody, from the boys to the graybeards.

Hot Springs took its first step toward becoming a community of large public institutions by securing the State Soldiers' Home, which was built at the head of Minnekahta Avenue on land originally belonging to Fred Evans, and finished in the summer of '90.

The South Dakota State Soldiers' Home was built for South Dakota resident veterans. This is the first building, constructed in 1889. In 2021 it contains the Michael J. Fitzmaurice VIP room (decorated with period pieces from the Pioneer Museum), meeting rooms, and staff housing.

It will be remembered that Dr. Stewart's "big house" at the Plunge site in 1882, was of logs. The Minnekahta Hotel, built in 1886, was of Black Hills pine lumber. The State Home marked what was the third—and should be the ultimate—stage in the town's building materials. It was solidly constructed of the pink native sandstone taken from the quarry on the Evans ranch near the Falls.

Later the Burke Quarry was opened, just down the canyon, furnishing a stone of buff color but similar texture, and fortunately nearly every public building erected in town since '89 has been of these beautiful and enduring materials.

Evans Quarry was on the north side of Fall River Road four miles east of Hot Springs. The cut rock wall is still visible on the north side of the highway.

Aside from its unusual topography and surroundings, this native building stone is the thing which gives Hot Springs its distinctive appearance in the eye of a stranger. Nearly all other small towns seem to have been made wholesale at some huge central factory and shipped to their present locations. Their business blocks are of monotonously similar brick—the favorite brick of the moment being rough faced and the color of a dried beef liver; their school buildings are of brick, trimmed with artificial stone; the Court House, if any, is shipped from Indiana. In this day of heavy motor travel every small town has to be elaborately labeled where the highways enter it, because it looks just like every other town for the past five hundred miles.

Madame Standardization, that efficient but dull fairy godmother who is so powerful today, has waved her leaden wand over the country and made our towns, like our clothes, stupidly uniform.

Not so Hot Springs. A blindfolded man, landed in the canyon from afar by airplane, would, as he snatched off the bandage

A close up of the Fargo-Dickover building shows the carving detail in the locally quarried sandstone.

and his eye caught sight of the nearest large building, say: "This is Hot Springs." The town's stone buildings look solid and dignified, yet the cheerful tints of the native rock save them from that tomb-like impression presented by so many

This photo shows Fred Evans' freighting company when it was stopped near Buffalo Gap. Evans quit freighting and sold his company during 1885 or 1886.

public structures elsewhere, expensively built out of the sad-colored standard bricks and stones.

Of the officials of the Company in 1886 it is to be noted that two—Stewart and Jennings—were physicians, one—Dudley, was a lawyer, and one—Evans—was a capitalist. This was a well balanced recipe for leadership in a town of the sort Hot Springs aspired to be. Now, as then, by far the greater number of the town's professional men are physicians, as is right, and the law is also well represented. Hot Springs of today, though, could use a few more public-spirited capitalists of the Evans type.

The Hot Springs House, also known as Hot Springs Hotel, was shown with the Minnekahta Bathhouse adjacent. In 2019 the Moccasin Springs Natural Mineral Spa was constructed on the same site.

When the Elkhorn had laid its track to within a stone's throw of Deadwood, Fred Evans disposed of the huge freighting outfits by which he had been supplying the mining district

The original Evans Plunge as it looked when built in 1890; it remained in operation in 2021.

with everything from dry goods and groceries to steam boilers and stamp mills, and thereafter gave his whole energy and capital to the building up of Hot Springs. He built the Hot Springs Hotel, then called the Sanitarium, and enclosed the old squaw's tub in an adequate bath house.

He considered the Lakota group of springs at the upper end of town, and built the [Evans] Plunge, which has always been one of the great attractions of the place.

He built the still beautiful Minnekahta Block, and numerous lesser structures. He built and graded many of the streets of the upper town at his own expense. He used every ounce of influence which his previous large business operations had given him in the older parts of the country, to advertise and promote the new health resort.

He was seconded by a group of very eager men, some pioneers and some newcomers, but all equally enthusiastic as to the possibilities of the Springs. The development of Upper Town as a business district ran counter to the old plans, and for some time there was considerable friction between the up-canyon section and Lower Town—so much so that for a

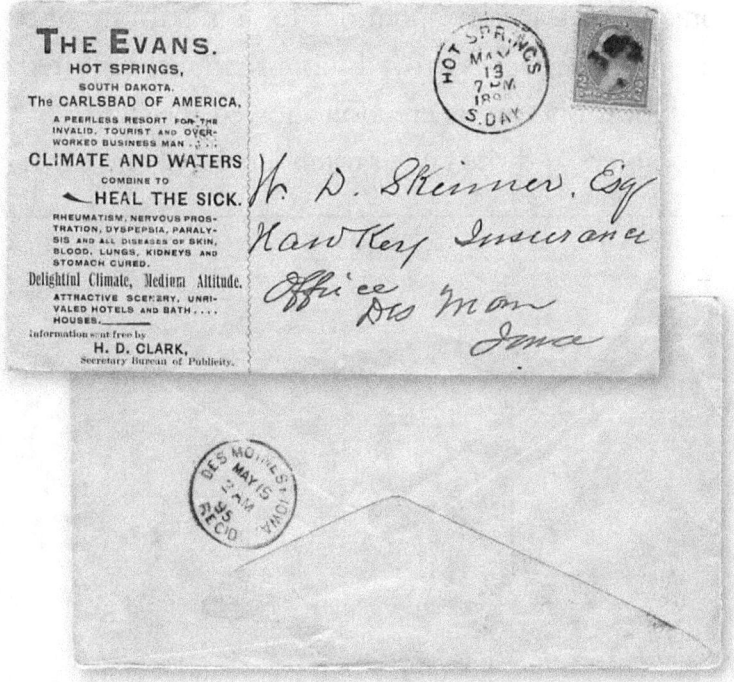

This letter, written on promotional business stationery, was mailed May 13, 1895. The letter was received in Des Moines two days later, May 15, 1895.

while Upper and Lower Towns threatened to pull apart and develop a Minneapolis-and-St. Paul state of mind but luckily this has been forgotten, except as a minor incident in history. The handsome Gillespie Hotel was built on the bank of the river adjoining Minnekahta Avenue, and was balanced in Lower Town by the Fargo and Dickover building at Seventh and Chicago Avenue—both of them now long ago gone up in smoke, but notable structures in their day. During the summer of '90 the town opened its third bank.

Another major event of 1890 was the completion and opening of Black Hills College, a Methodist institution, on what had been the old Stewart homestead. The large and sightly building of native stone with its accommodations for a maximum of two hundred students, afterwards proved more than was required for its day and location, but its erection showed the limitless faith of its promoters and the cultural tendencies of the town.

The Gillespie Hotel was under construction in this 1890 photo; it burned December 23, 1915.

Its establishment was hailed with satisfaction, not only by Hot Springs but by the whole Hills. "Let us send our children to our own college," said the *Sturgis Record*, "instead of shipping them back east to be filled up with dude ideas, Yankee notions and malaria."

The Black Hills College was short-lived. It opened September 11, 1890 and closed at the end of the college year May 25, 1900. The city purchased the building to use as the high school in 1910. It burned in 1924.

This Hot Springs High School was built on the former college location after the college burned in 1924. The new (and currently in use in 2021) high school was ready for students in September 1925.

The institution was opened in the fall of '90 with an initial enrollment of twenty-four students. After a few years, being ahead of its time, it had to close but, as is often remarked, it did its work well while it lived, for the old students of Black Hills College, scattered now from coast to coast, are in all cases respected people and a credit to their deceased alma mater. The college building, after standing unused for some years, was bought by the city and made into a high school, serving thus until it was destroyed by fire and replaced by the beautiful new high school building.

All that remains of the college now is the name of one section of the city—College Hill.

In 1890 the Minnekahta Hotel—the "new" Minnekahta only four years before, but now, in the accelerated rate of the

The Presbyterian Church on Happy Hollow is now a private residence.

town's progress, already the "old" Minnekahta—took fire and its 150,000 feet of well seasoned Black Hills pine lumber made a grand conflagration. This fire, which would have been a calamity of the first magnitude only a year or two before, hardly caused a ripple in the swift days of '90, but just served to clear an excellent building site, upon which Fred Evans fixed a calculating eye.

Religion kept pace with business in the boom, and during '90 the Baptist and Presbyterian congregations both completed new houses of worship, the former on College Hill and the latter in Happy Hollow.

Also this was the year of the first chautauqua. In those days. Chautauqua was a purveyor of education instead of popular entertainment, and was a much more important institution

The Chautauqua grounds were the site of rousing, week-long educational programs. This 1890 photo show the rail line and the buildings that accommodated the crowds.
W.R.Cross Photo

than it is now. The first Hot Springs assembly was held in September 1890, at the romantic spot up Hot Brook Canyon, which is still known as the Chautauqua grounds, and the following year extensive improvements made the place an ideal location for such an outdoor educational project.

It was so used for several years, and enjoyed not only by the townspeople but by sojourners from all over the Hills. In the very height of its business boom, Hot Springs was able to appreciate learning and the finer things of life.

In July of the great year of '90 this settlement in the canyon of the warm springs, which we have been dignifying by the name of "town" all through this story, really became a town. It was incorporated as a third-class city. There was an election in July to determine the will of the citizenry in the matter, but apparently nobody voted no, so the new State of South Dakota acquired the new City of Hot Springs. In August the first city election was held. *The Star*—which was taken with an acute spurt of ambition about this time and began to publish *The Daily Star*—reported that "the election passed off quietly." The first mayor of Hot Springs was J. B. Dickover. The city council consisted of F. D. Gillespie, R. F. Connor, R. D. Jennings, Wm. Crane, W. W. Root and Henry Marty. The treasurer was A. S. Stewart.

These first city fathers, in their lively, half-built community, had a vast number of things to consider. One matter was the organization of a fire company. The buildings of the town were now valuable enough and close enough together so that fire was a real hazard. Men for the proposed fire department were plentiful, but there was nothing for them to fight fire with. The town had

On October 11, 1903 the row of wooden buildings across from the Union Depot burned with losses of $12,850.00. The replacements, including the Minnekahta Block, were locally quarried sandstone.
Horan Collection

no water works. Water was hauled in barrels from the springs to the homes, or obtained from wells. A fire engine with a suction hose in the creek might have solved the problem, but fire engines were very expensive pieces of furniture and the city fathers had as yet little money to spend, so the citizens for a spell took it out in discussion, meanwhile looking to their chimney flues and handling their pipes and cigars and kerosene lamps with care.

But the town grew. How it did grow! The *Star*, during the fall started a wrangle with the *Rapid City Journal* as to which town had done the most building for the year. The argument was never definitely settled but, as those were also boom days in Rapid, which has always outclassed Hot Springs in size, it is a good gauge of the health-town's growth at that period.

"We used to know everybody in town," writes the editor of the *Star*, half plaintively, "but during this year we have completely lost track." Truly the figures for the year are impressive. In December 1889, the population was 583. In the same month of 1890 it was, in round numbers, 1,500.

The sandstone for the new buildings came from Fred Evans' quarry. Evans Quarry was on the north side of Fall River Road four miles east of Hot Springs. The cut rock wall is still visible on the north side of the highway.

The epochal year of 1890 was also the one in which Hot Springs saw the last of the Wild West. Rumors of an Indian outbreak, heard so many times during the past ten years, finally proved well-founded. That fall the last Indian war in United States history carried terror almost within rifle shot of town.

The old fighting Sioux, snatched from the very simple life which they and their fathers had lived since time was young, and pitched neck and crop into a civilization so complicated that it often puzzles us who were born to it, were hopelessly bewildered and miserable. In this condition they fell victims to a dream which has so often lured unhappy captives—the dream of a Messiah who should conquer their enemies and restore their former glories. This Messiah was to blot out the whites by miraculous means; the vanished buffalo were to reappear on the plains in greater numbers than ever, and the red sons of the Great Spirit were to resume their splendid, carefree sportsman's life of hunting and fighting where the fair skinned invaders had interrupted it a few years before. It is not for us to make fun of this dream. Considerable numbers of our white brethren prepare for the end of the world, and even fix the exact date, every year or two. Our white ancestors all over Europe went crazy on a religious idea during the Crusades, and stayed crazy for a matter of four hundred years. There are dozens of such instances in white history, far more absurd than the Sioux Messiah craze of 1890.

A means of spiritual purification and preparation for the expected advent of the red Messiah was the Ghost Dance, a religious rite in which warriors danced until they were exhausted and, falling into a mystic trance, were supposed to receive supernatural revelations. This dance was freely practiced and aroused great excitement among the Indians on the Reservation, and may have been the main cause of the hostilities that followed. Whether the latter could have been handled more wisely by the white authorities is not for this story to discuss. No doubt the management of those fierce red children was a job to tax the keenest diplomatic mind, yet as a

General Miles and staff were photographed at the Pine Ridge Indian camp on January 16, 1891.
John C. H. Grabill photo

race we have never been famous for the delicacy and sympathy with which we have treated peoples with darker skins, once they were in our power. At any rate, trouble began. Despite the counsels of the more thoughtful and intelligent Indians, parties of reckless young braves broke out of the Reservation and ranged the country, mainly with the object of stealing horses, which had always been considered a praiseworthy military feat in tribal warfare. Some groups, flaunting the old-time panoply of paint and feathers but armed now with rifles, penetrated even into the piney gulches of the Hills themselves. There were some killings, and each killing bred rumor of twenty more.

Pine Ridge Indian camp as it stood on January 16, 1891.
W. R. Cross photo

The Government acted and regular troops poured into the western part of the State.

The Hills towns, safe because of their numbers, regarded the matter as rather a bore, and even thought the amount of fuss was out of proportion to the trouble. The isolated ranchman, however, worried about his scalp and his livestock, and perhaps desperately anxious about a wife and children, took a different view. He could hardly speak of the campaign of "masterly inactivity" conducted by General Miles from Rapid City without profane intensives.

Hot Springs did not seem upset about experiencing both a boom and a war in a single year. Whatever it may have said about the war in private conversation, the town was officially calm and conservative. The *Star*, in protesting against the sensational reports of the trouble in city papers, advanced the opinion that those "envious Eastern sheets" had seized upon this little Indian flurry as a chance to misrepresent South Dakota and scare tourists and investors away from the Hills—a complaint which has quite an up-to-date sound. The town, with its fifteen hundred people, had no fears for itself, but felt itself bound to offer what protection it could to the ranch people in the territory, so a military company was formed, with M. L. Kanable as captain. Procuring arms, they began regular drill and held themselves ready to move at an hour's notice, should a call for help come from the range.

The ranchmen also organized, and a regular patrol of keen-eyed and heavily armed riders was established along the Cheyenne. At the Jack Daly ranch a party of Sioux ran off a bunch of horses, without casualties. The cowboys, bent on revenge, sent two men with a fresh band of horses to the place in broad daylight. The Indians observed this movement with covetous eyes, but they failed to see a dozen more men who stole to the place in the darkness of the following night. The Sioux came at dawn, as was their custom, and attempted to clean out the corral, whereat the house spouted fire and thunder from between its logs and the braves left hastily, minus the horses and leaving several of their number sprawled dead on the buffalo grass.

William (Bill) Wyatt was an early county pioneer. He came from Stafford, England when he was 17. He worked on the Bar T ranch until he qualified as a cowboy.

Bill Wyatt tells of war conditions while he was living at his ranch on the Cheyenne, at the mouth of Shep's Canyon.

There were five families in the neighborhood, and they concentrated at one ranch for mutual protection. Of course the house was intolerably crowded, and during the first night a child was born there. On the next morning Mrs. Wyatt announced that Indians or no Indians, she was going home, so she and her husband once more took their chances alone in their own house. A day or two after that, in the midst of a furious winter storm, the first Wyatt child was born. As has been said before, the greater part of the praise we bestow upon the hardy pioneer should be reserved for the hardy pioneer's womenfolk.

The last Indian war was a matter of only a few months, though to people whose interest in it was so personal as these just mentioned, it must have seemed much longer. It culminated in the sickening slaughter of Indians of all ages and both sexes at Wounded Knee, and the death of Sitting Bull, shot by a reservation policeman of his own race. In the early months of '91 the disillusioned red men, finding that their Messiah did not come and that the White man's war medicine was stronger than ever, came in and surrendered.

It is only fair to notice that since that last pitiful outbreak, the record of the Oglala Sioux has been admirable. The excellent government schools, with the co-operation of the Indians themselves, have produced a fine new generation of red people. There seems always to have been a strong religious streak in the Sioux psychology and it is remarkable that these people—one of the fiercest of all the warlike tribes in American history and the tribe which won the most complete victory ever gained by Indians over white soldiers, at the Custer fight—took wholeheartedly to the gentle precepts of Christianity, once they had definitely abandoned their old ways. Today the percentage of church membership among them is vastly higher than it is among whites. They still visit Hot Springs, the health resort of their forefathers, and are always welcome. They are a people of many fine qualities and will furnish a valuable ingredient toward that most interesting blend, the eventual American.

Chapter 8
The End of the Trail

Buffalo Gap had enjoyed a boom. Edgemont, on the new Burlington, was beginning to develop delusions of grandeur and strain its vest buttons. Oelrichs thought remarkably well of itself. While as yet Hot Springs was the biggest town in the county, there was no certainty, in those expansive days, that it would remain so. It was thought wise to fix the county seat in the canyon permanently by the erection of a real court house. To this end a bond election was held in February, 1891. The returns from Hot Springs and Oelrichs in this election are interesting in view of their divergent notions about the location of the county seat a few years before. Hot Springs rolled up 597 votes for the bonds and just one lonely ballot against them.

The Fall River County Court House was constructed in 1891 and continues to serve the county in 2021.

Oelrichs, on the other hand, cast just two votes in favor of the bonds and 100 against. The vote indicates that the Oelrichs of that day was full of die-hards, and also guarantees that there was nothing crooked, this time, about the ballot boxes in the two towns. So the court house was built—native stone, of course and at that time was by far the finest court house in all the Hills, and one of the finest in the state.

Rapid City will please refrain from snickering when it is stated that the building was completed at a cost of $25,000. As the boy said about the old story of athletic young George Washington throwing a coin across the Potomac, "a dollar went a heap further in those days."

A court house is always an interesting building. The jail is a place of blasted hopes and vain longings. The court room is the stage for many tragedies, though generally the most serious of them is not without its comic relief. The county offices, dealing as they do with the personal affairs of so many citizens, from marriage to murder, are a perfect magazine of concentrated, high-power gossip which might explode and blow the whole county to rags, socially, were they not guarded by the close-mouthed "courthouse gang." There are many court house stories—some of them sad, of course, some of them funny, but a large number of the mixed, tragi-comic variety. There is room for one of the last named sort here, and though it is "on" an excellent lady, it is too true to life to be omitted.

While C. S. Eastman was sheriff, in the nineties, an Indian named Thunder Hawk was in jail awaiting trial for murder and, Indian like, he was desperately unhappy in his confinement. Early one morning Mr. Eastman left the sheriff's quarters, then as now in the lower story of the court house, and went down town on an errand before breakfast. When he came back up the canyon, he saw his wife run out of their apartments, showing signs of excitement and distress, and as he hastened toward her she cried:

"Oh, come quick! Thunder Hawk has killed himself."

The sheriff dashed into the jail and found that the caged wild creature had tried to win a final freedom by using his large silk neckerchief to hang himself from the upper bars of his cell door. Eastman whipped out his knife and cut the Indian down, but a moment's examination showed that life had been extinct for some time. An hour later, when the flurry had subsided and they were at the breakfast table, the sheriff looked across at his wife curiously and asked:

"Why didn't you cut Thunder Hawk down yourself, when you found him?" "Because—" Mrs. Eastman hesitated, "because I wasn't sure he was dead."

In the spring of 1891 the favorite drive of the townspeople who owned or could hire a horse and buggy was down the canyon.

The canyon road, with its meandering course and its frequent fordings of the gay little river, was then even more romantic than it is now, but it was the romance of human achievement rather than that of mountain scenery which drew the excursionists. The Elkhorn was coming. The right of way through Lower Town had actually been secured. That right of way, as it happened, wiped out one notable bit of private property. It went squarely through the middle of Dr. Stewart's watermelon patch, a piece of soil of such excellence that it

An excursion on the canyon road [Fall River Road] in horse and buggy was a common pastime.

Arundel C. Hull photo, Eugene Arundel Hull Collection

was locally famous for growing watermelons too huge for even the husky boys of Hot Springs to steal. But this loss, serious as it was, faded into oblivion as the townsmen watched the perspiring gangs, with their work train pushed up by a leisurely, smoking locomotive at their heels, spiking down the last of the steel which was to bind Hot Springs to the great world beyond the hills.

The extensions of the Elkhorn and the Burlington into the Black Hills had throughout their construction been a matter of hot rivalry between the two roads, and this rivalry was still noticeable in the building of the Hot Springs branches. The Burlington had the bad luck to approach Hot Springs through a piece of country which, while charmingly picturesque, was well calculated to make an engineer swear, so the Elkhorn finally won the race by a nose. It was a grand day for the town

These were the two private cars that Robert Quayle, the superintendent of the Chicago Northwestern Railway, his wife and entourage used when they traveled to Hot Springs in 1903.
Horan Collection

when the first Elkhorn train whistled in and set the startled echoes to whooping down the canyon and along the piney slopes of the Seven Sisters Range. The engine was decked with flags and the whole town turned out to meet it. Hot Springs has since been hostess to a thousand excursions, but none of them ever got a more enthusiastic welcome than did the few passengers on that first train.

The Burlington came in with an equal amount of noise about a

The two railroads built a depot in cooperation making an elegant Union Depot. The wooden buildings across the street denote the photo was taken before the October 11, 1903 fire.
Horan Collection

month later. After the tracks had actually reached the canyon, the peaceful influence of the place made itself felt, even in the iron bosoms of railway corporations, and today the two roads use the same station— "the smallest union depot in the world"—and their locomotives sizzle sociably side by side in a common engine house.

Fred Evans had for a year or more been turning the idea of a really big hotel over in his mind. It had been rumored that the hotel was to go up at the Sulphur Springs and various other sites, but finally the plans of the master-builder of Hot Springs fixed upon the ruins of the burned Minnekahta, located at the junction of the two main canyons and with a beautiful view straight up the newly graded Minnekahta Avenue, guarded on either hand by its pine-plumed hilltops. In the Evans Hotel its builder outdid himself, as he intended to. It was still a day of makeshift crudities in western South Dakota, but Mr. Evans put into the construction of his new hostelry every refinement and luxury known to the hotel architecture of that day. It was the finest hotel in the Hills when it was built, though Hot

The Evans Hotel was built during 1891 to 1892. Fred Evans with his white horse team, Frank and Charley, are on the left.
Frank Jay Haynes photo

Springs was as yet one of the smaller towns of the region.

How far it was in advance of its time is shown by the fact that, for a period of more than 35 years it has remained the finest hotel in the Hills. It was opened on the first of June 1892, and during the first ten years of its operation it really fixed the quality and standing of Hot Springs as a town.

And here my story is ended. With the coming of the railroad and the completion of the Evans, the pioneer period in Hot

The Nichols Cancer Sanitarium.

Springs closes. In a local sense, that was literally the end of the trail. Thereafter the direct, mathematical railway and highway were to take the place of the delightfully haphazard and meandering trails of the early days. In like manner the unscientific view of the springs as a half-magical "catholicon," panacea, infallible cure for all ills, was to give way to their use as a valuable remedial agent in connection with the latest and best medical practice. In '92 or thereabouts the development of Hot Springs became a business instead of an adventure. It is not necessary to tell the rest of the town's history at present. It is still fresh in the memory of many people, and has been adequately "written up" in a hundred places. The object of this imperfect sketch was just to catch some of the high lights of the romantic eighties, before the last of the old-timers crossed the divide and they faded out forever.

In the early nineties the fluid and uncertain destiny of Hot Springs "jellied," and it took the general lines of the town of today. Of course the population has doubled since then. The town has acquired two groups of physicians and surgeons of high standing, connected with two large and perfectly equipped hospitals. The waters of the springs still do their work in bath houses where the latest scientific knowledge supervises the treatments.

The Nichols Cancer Sanitarium was one of the early hospitals. For many years it was a nursing home known as Castle Manor. In December 2014, the residents moved into a new home, Seven Sisters Living Center, adjacent to the newly-constructed Fall River Health Services hospital and clinic. The building was sold at auction and in 2021, it is under renovation for residential living space, and is simply called The Castle.

The government has built Battle Mountain Sanitarium, a vast and beautiful hospital and home for the veteran soldiers of all the states, and the hospital practice of the State Home, as well as its membership, has been greatly extended.

The sandstone Catholicon Bathhouse/hotel sat at the foot of the Seven Sisters, before the bathhouse was destroyed by fire.

W. R. Cross photo

The Siloam Bathhouse was constructed on the Catholicon site and the house was where the Orlando Ferguson family lived.

Hot Springs of today is a full-fledged health resort, but it is only a natural growth from what was well begun in 1890. The summer brings the town hosts of pleasure- seekers, coming now mostly in the automobile instead of the long excursion trains of the nineties, and Hot Springs has become the great convention town of South Dakota, but this is only the working out of the dreams of Evans and Dudley and Stewart and Jennings in the old, old days.

Battle Mountain Sanitarium, later named the Veterans Administration hospital, was completed in 1907. The VA is still open for veterans' care in 2021.

In fact, the character of the place was fixed even before Turner and Trimmer and Dennis and Petty drifted into the canyon. The purple and saffron splashes in the canyon formations, backed by the deep pervading red of soil and rock and the dark green of the pines, pleased the barbaric taste of the first Indians who ever drank the clear water of the little river. The waters themselves delighted the old squaw because they made her comfortable and well. There is the destiny of Hot Springs to make people happy and well—surely no unworthy mission.

In considering the early days of the place the idea of a pup was irresistible, and led to the title of this sketch. The hamlet in those days was like a pup—good-natured and well-intentioned and with unmistakable thoroughbred points, yet so wildly playful and with a tendency to tumble over itself in its undertakings. That metaphor can be abandoned now for something human. Lead, the Homestake town, can be personified as a broad-backed, Amazonian woman, digging out the treasures of the earth. Spearfish is something between a farmer girl and a school ma'am. Rapid is a curt, efficient business woman, but Hot Springs from the first was fated to be a hostess and a belle. Beauty and charm may be regarded by other towns as incidentals or luxuries, but Hot Springs will never dare to be caught with her nose shiny or her heels run over. An important part of her work in healing the sick and recreating the tired vacationist is that she should always appear trim and smiling. Beauty is her business. This has always been in the minds of her builders, and should continue to govern her growth as each nail is driven and each stone laid.

The high spots in Hot Springs' career as a hostess arrived in the summer of 1927, when the President of the United States and his lady came to call. There were many distinguished names among her collection of calling cards, but this was the first time that a President had ever crossed her threshold, and even though Presidents should become commonplace in the future, 1927 will always be remembered. River Avenue, after forty-five years, was no longer a buffalo trail winding down the canyon, but a fair street, broad, well paved, flanked on one side by business houses and on the other by a line of shade trees

North River Street had tree-lined streets in this circa 1938 photo. The cars range from 1932 to 1938.

Stevens Studio Photo

and the rushing creek, its warm waters still as limpidly clear as on the day it was discovered by the Indians. The street was swept clear of traffic for the occasion, and guarded by soldiers of the local company of Engineers, not through any fear for the President's safety but for reasons of state and ceremony.

President and Mrs. Coolidge were at Battle Mountain Sanitarium and toured Hot Springs on August 18, 1927.

Stevens Studio Photo

When Hot Springs Was A Pup

A line of shining automobiles, driven by Hot Springs citizens, met the president and his party of distinguished people at the Union Station and bore them smoothly away over the pavement. (How the "magnificent tally-ho coaches" with their laboring fours used to come straining and pitching through the red mud from Buffalo Gap!) A swift ride up the incline that climbs the east wall of the canyon above the roofs of the business district, and the presidential party were swept into the lovely grounds of Battle Mountain Sanitarium, where, drawn up on the broad lawns before the administration building, the veteran soldiers of many states waited to receive the Commander-in-chief.

The 7th Street bridge was over Fall River at the base of the road to College Hill, before the viaduct. In 1934 the original viaduct was constructed as a U.S. Public Works project.

(Military ground, this, since that day when a cloud of red dust rose from pony hoofs and the canyon below echoed to battle

President and Mrs. Coolidge along with their entourage enjoyed Hot Springs. In 1927, the summer White House was located in the Black Hills.

Stevens Studio photo

cries, and Sioux arrows whizzed and Cheyenne lances bickered in the sun and the buffalo grass was dyed crimson with Indian blood, a century and a half ago.) Then down the canyon again and along the shady length of River Avenue, up Eighth Street and along Chicago Avenue (once Petty's cornfield) over the Seventh Street bridge and up the winding road to College Hill (from whose crest the '86ers used to count thirteen log cabins in the town) past the white walls of the high school, and up the wide, winding highway to the Country Club, on its hilltop among the pines.

The Coolidge party exited the SD State Veterans' Home after a tour on August 18, 1927.

Stevens Studio photo

There Hot Springs served luncheon to her honored guests, and at a little distance Hot Springs' own military band played among the trees. There was no formality. High-salaried correspondents of metropolitan newspapers forgot their eternal 'copy" and laughingly drove golf balls from the first tee to the velvety fairways far below, while Senators, Congressmen and even the President and his gracious lady mingled with the crowd on the veranda in neighborly familiarity. (A far cry from the rough board floors and the jingling spurs and Matt Bingham's fiddle, but the same spirit abides forever about the Springs.)

Then to the State Soldiers' Home, and a pause on the veranda there, looking down the winding gulch where Hot Springs history began and over the sweeping vista of the town—gulch and hilltop, splashes of red canyon wall and bits of lifting conglomerate cliff, masses of forest green, varying from the fresh tint of cottonwood to the black of pines. All this an Indian of old might have recognized but now, scattered everywhere among the hills were the walls and roofs of Hot Springs, with the great buildings of the Sanitarium gleaming on their emerald hilltop against the imposing general background of Battle Mountain.

Beauty! The befeathered, wandering savage saw it and made the canyon a shrine. Turner and Trimmer and the Pettys, drifting in from far, saw it and made the canyon a home. Evans and Jennings and Dudley and Stewart saw it and made the canyon a city. Forty years later a President of the United States, careless for the moment of the iron schedule which governs his days, saw it and lingered using his eyes. And Hot Springs of 1927, well pleased, drew away from the great man and left him alone to smoke thoughtfully as his gaze wandered across the parklike stretches of the hills, along the green slopes of the Seven Sisters and down to the walls of the little city nestled along the canyon at Battle Mountain's foot. This charmed lingering of the greatest ruler on earth might well mark the close of the first half-century of the town's history.

God did divinely well by the canyon of the warm springs. In the days since the skin tepees were pitched beside the springs, man has well supplemented God's work. And in man's hands rests the canyon's future.

Hometown
Badger Clark in *Scribner's Magazine*, October 1926

Our town has history enough.
Across the railroad, on the bluff
Prof scans the record of our age
And reads it, page by stony page.
Desert, he says, and swamp and sea
And glacier in turn were we.
The three-toed horse, he says, was here;
Rhinoceros and six-horned deer
And other strange and varied meats
Snorted and stamped about our streets
Back when the first town site survey
Was still a million years away.
And then the red man's pedigree,
With pigeon-toed solemnity,
Stalked through our annals in a string
And held their feasts beside our spring
Till old Jed Towner built his hut

Badger Clark

With one hand on a pistol butt.
Can Pontiac,
Kish or Karnak
Push their backgrounds further back?
Our town has sights as fine to see
As any in geography.
Why, when early sunlight spills
In summer down our eastern hills,
They look like heaven's parapet.
From Eighth Street, when the sun has set.
The high school on the hill in line
Looms like a castle on the Rhine.
And twisted pines along the crest
Backed by lemon-colored west
Would make Jap artists praise their gods
And plant their easels here by squads.
Some summer nights I have to lie
In the front yard and watch the sky,
And let my fancy climb and play
Through lacework of the Milky Way
To deeper heights all silver fired.
Until both eyes and brain are tired.
Oh, never Nome,
Hongkong or Rome
Could show me finer sights than home!

Hot Springs Characters

Badger Clark

Hot Springs has always been an asylum for the weak, but it has been built and maintained by exceptionally strong men. Hot Springs history is full of "characters" not mere eccentrics, but men of personality and power.

Dr. R. D. Jennings was the fifth head of family to land on the town site—in the fall of '81. He was the first hotel keeper and the first hospital physician, his hospital and hotel being a long, low, mud-daubed log cabin. Nearby one of the springs fell into a natural bath tub, partly eroded by water and partly chipped out of living rock by generations of Indians. Here Dr. Jennings treated the first patients at the Black Hills spa, frequently carrying them to the rock tub in his arms.

Dr. A. S. Stewart brought the sixth family to the remote and dangerous canyon of the warm waters. He was an associate of Jennings and the two were probably responsible for fixing the destiny of the town as a health resort above all else. From '82 on, Dr. Stewart planned, lived and dreamed Hot Springs for thirty years. He at one time owned what is now College Hill as a homestead, but he cut it up into lots and offered it at liberal terms, that is, he agreed to make a present of a lot to anybody who would build on it.

Fred Evans was the master-builder of old Hot Springs. He had made a fortune in various kinds of transportation, ranging from street cars in Sioux City to "bull" freight outfits between Pierre and Deadwood. After the railroad reached Deadwood he gave his whole time, energy and fortune to the building up of Hot Springs, and has left his mark everywhere on the town. Mr. Evans was a bearded giant, an ideal pioneer type, and some of the stories of his energy and determination have almost passed into legend. Like nearly all the old timers, he died in the town he loved.

C. L. (Chris) Jensen entered Hot Springs in 1883, and for many years thereafter was famous as a horseman and story teller. Mr. Jensen has never aspired to literary honors but many of his stories of pioneer life used to raise the hair or the risibilities of passengers on his Wind Cave stages. He maintained the largest livery and stage establishment in Hot Springs, during the horse era and when the horse went the way of the ox-team, Mr. Jensen took up another line of communication and became manager for the telephone company in Hot Springs. In addition to this he is now (1928) major of the city.

A. W. (Archie) Riordan was town marshal in Buffalo Gap at the time the railroad reached there in the '80s. This alone is proof of his courage and force of character, for the Gap sowed bushels of the wildest kind of oats during those years. For a long time he has been proprietor of the Hot Springs Bottling Works and one of the leading business men of the town. Like most of the men who had a part in taming the Wild West, Mr. Riordan is a quiet-spoken gentleman of a thoughtful and philosophical turn of mind.

Ellis T. (Doc) Peirce belonged in a measure to the whole Hills, being one of the earliest pioneers of Deadwood and Custer, but his many years' residence in the canyon of the warm waters gives Hot Springs the right to claim him. As his writings indicate, twenty-five years of Mr. Peirce's life were a perfect epic of adventure, and there were few persons or events in the history of the Old West that he was not familiar with. The many friends of his quieter years in Hot Springs remember him as an excellent citizen, a lovable friend and the most entertaining company in the world.

John G. (Johnnie) Richer rode into Fall River County in the early '80s as a cowpuncher helping to chaperone a large herd of longhorns up the long trail from Kansas. For some time after that he filled a saddle for the WG Outfit and was once, during his range years, a side-kick of Jim Dahlman, who has since become the almost chronic mayor of Omaha. Mr. Richer's marriage was one of the early social events of Hot Springs and he is the father of a large and creditable family. Physically he is a whippet model, but with plenty of power, and is still as cheerily active as ever about his business affairs.

Eben W. Martin, probably the finest political figure which the Black Hills had produced, was for many years a Deadwood attorney and Congressman from the third district, but his large property interests connected him closely with Hot Springs even before he took up his residence there ten years ago. Mr. Martin has never used his prominence and power selfishly and Hot Springs has many things to thank him for, the greatest of these being his part in securing the Battle Mountain Sanitarium for the town during his days in Washington, and the later use of his influence to wrest the tubercular unit of the same institution from so powerful a competitor as the city of Minneapolis. He is never niggardly of time and energy spent for the good of the community.

U. S. G. (Grant) Robinson, like many of the long-time residents of Hot Springs, knows the feel of a horse and the look of a steer, and used to twirl a mean lariat. Mr. Robinson accumulated a comfortable fortune in cattle, most of which is now invested in Hot Springs property. He was an energetic mayor of the city for four years, during which time a large paving program and many other public improvements were put through. And he is still building.

Captain C. V. Gardner has been an honored member of the State Home for a number of years, so Hot Springs claims him, though he is better known as "The Grand Old Man of the Black Hills." Captain Gardner started the first newspaper in the Black Hills, shipped in the first carload of goods, introduced the first quartz mill and has several other "firsts" in Black Hills history to his credit. He has always been a man of exceptional energy, a dreamer and a doer of the true pioneer type. When he was nearly ninety years old, he disregarded physical infirmities and traveled alone all over the Hills for several months, raising the money to build the monument to Annie D. Tallent near Custer. And his grip on life and life's affairs is still as strong and hearty as his handclasp.

G. Carroll Smith built section corners, dodged Indians and shot buffalo all over the present State of Wyoming during the early days. Later he married and settled at Buffalo Gap during the boom days of that town. For many years, however, he has been a well-known and well-liked citizen of Hot Springs. "Bank of Hot Springs" is Carroll Smith's other name, and has been ever since that solid institution was in its swaddling clothes. Oddly enough, Carroll's great passion, aside from the honest handling of other people's money, is the cultivation of flowers, and his yard for years has been one of the show places of the town.

Dr. C. W. Hargens is another man of energy whose name has been connected with Hot Springs for more years, perhaps, than he would care to have told. At once adventurous and level-headed, Dr. Hargens long ago won the reputation of being one of the most daring, yet safe and skillful, surgeons in half-a-dozen states, and has always kept in the front ranks of that exacting and swiftly- changing profession. For several terms he was mayor of Hot Springs, and put into that job the same qualities that made him famous in his own vocation. Dr. Hargens' hair and beard are now white, but to one who sees him daily about his practice it seems that Nature must have made a slip in scattering the snows of time on so youthful a man.

W. H. (Walt) Knowlton reached Deadwood in '80, moved to Buffalo Gap in '85, and from there to Hot Springs in '91, so he is a Black Hiller of long standing. Mr. Knowlton is one of those men as systematic as the movement of the stars and as regular as the cycle of the seasons. He came to Hot Springs as manager of the Chase clothing business, of which he later became the proprietor, and his success is proof of the wisdom of taking one line and sticking to it. Kennett Harris, in his inimitable Saturday Evening Post stories, often uses the name of Walt Knowlton. It is thirty-odd years since Mr. Harris left Hot Springs, so Walt Knowlton, besides being a successful business man, is a friend not easily forgotten.

C. S. (Charlie) Eastman was a citizen of Oelrichs at the time in the eighties when that town contested the county seat with

Hot Springs. He was loyal to Oelrichs through that battle, but when the dust had settled and the dead were buried, his profession, the law, drew him to Hot Springs and Hot Springs has had him ever since. Mr. Eastman served as sheriff in the nineties and those who know him best say he is quite as dangerous on the other end of a six-shooter as he is on the other end of a legal argument, which is a strong statement. He was also postmaster under the Wilson administration. The Hot Springs climate has had its usual effect in this case, and nobody would suspect Charlie Eastman of being past thirty-five if he did not betray himself by early-day reminiscences.

Many other names occur to one familiar with the citizenry of Hot Springs, but the lack of space puts an end to these "thumbnail sketches." The town in the canyon of the warm springs has never been very rich in money but it has always been rich in men.

Editors' notes on the text

Linda M. Hasselstrom and Peggy A. Sanders

Badger Clark continued to refer to the town as Minnekahta even after the town was officially named Hot Springs in 1883; in addition, he says the change of names was made in 1886.

Fall River County Commissioners minutes book 1, page 1. Jennie and Edmund (Ted) Petty donated the plot of land that was the first official site of Hot Springs. They had the land surveyed and on January 31, 1883, the first platted lots of Hot Springs were filed, under the 'Town of Hot Springs.' They dedicated the streets and alleys of the plat "to the use and benefit of the public." On November 17, 1883, Fall River County was established "In accordance with a Commission issued by the Governor of Dakota Territory," that Edmund Petty, Elisha P. Chilson, and Wm. P. Phillips be named the first Fall River County Commissioners. John Hills, a Notary Public in and for Custer County, "qualified" the three men as commissioners; they then held an election of officers. Edmund Petty was chosen chairman and E. P. Chilson, secretary. A motion was made by Edmund Petty that Hot Springs be made the county seat of Fall River County, Dakota Territory, which was unanimously approved.

He often wrote the date without including the century designation. It is important to remember that a reference to '81 means 1881.

When Badger refers to "the Plunge," he is speaking about the spring on the south side of the current Minnekahta Avenue, where the moccasin-shaped bathtub is located, not Evans Plunge.

Badger's prose book, *Spike*, is based on his ranch stay in Arizona and each of the short chapters is extremely funny. *The Hermosa News* of August 7, 1914, refers to the Jack Daly ranch as being "near the Cheyenne River." *Last Grass Frontier*, the history of the South Dakota Stock Growers Association by Bob Lee and Dick Williams, indicates the ranch was at the mouth of Battle Creek.

Badger Clark refers to National Heights which is the location of Battle Mountain Sanitarium, now called the Veterans Administration hospital.

The Burlington and Missouri River Railroad (B&MR) was an American railroad company incorporated in Iowa in 1852, with headquarters in Omaha, Nebraska. It was developed to build a railroad across the state of Iowa, beginning operations in 1856. It was acquired by the Chicago, Burlington and Quincy Railroad in 1872 and kept serving as its subsidiary.

The Seven Sisters Range, a sub-range of the Black Hills, lies southeast of Hot Springs. See **summitpost.org**, for more information.

"Hot Springs Characters" by Badger Clark was found in the collection of the Pioneer Museum in Hot Springs, S.D., by Peggy A. Sanders. To our knowledge it has not been published before, so it seems especially appropriate to include it here.

The name Badger was a family name. It was the maiden name of the mother of Charles Badger Clark, Sr. who generally went by C. B. Clark or Reverend Clark. The poet and author went by Charlie while growing up. His early poetry in *Pacific*

Monthly was submitted under the name C. B. Clark, Jr. Seeking to alleviate confusion, he settled on using simply Badger Clark.

Scribner's Magazine was an American periodical issued by the publishing house of Charles Scribner's Sons from January 1887 to May 1939. *Scribner's Magazine* was the second magazine out of the Scribner's firm, after the publication of *Scribner's Monthly*. Charles Scribner's Sons spent over $500,000 setting up the magazine, to compete with the already successful *Harper's Monthly* and *The Atlantic Monthly*. *Scribner's Magazine* was launched in 1887, and was the first of any magazine to introduce color illustrations. The magazine ceased publication in 1939.

Additional magazines in which Badger's writing was published include: *Pacific Monthly, Sunset, Collier's, Century Magazine, Ladies Home Journal, Outlook, Literary Digest, Survey, Pasque Petals, South Dakota Library Bulletin, The Teepee Book, Poetry: A Magazine of Verse, Christian Century, The Rotarian* and *Outing,* an outdoor sporting and cycling magazine published from the 1882 to 1923, with four title changes over those years.

Afterword: Slingin' Ink and English

Linda M. Hasselstrom

My contact with Badger Clark was brief and mostly consisted of an exchange of letters, but his influence on my life has been huge.

My mother gave me my first copy of *Sun and Saddle Leather* in 1955, when I was twelve years old. I read, memorized and then recited the poems at the slightest excuse from then on. In 1958, my grandmother Cora Hey, who never had an opportunity for much education, gave me #252 of an edition of *Sky Lines and Wood Smoke* which was limited to 1000 copies.

During my childhood, I also read Badger's poems in the *Custer County Chronicle*, to which my father always subscribed. The *Chronicle* was then published by Jessie (Mrs. Carl H.) Sundstrom. I doubt if she ever rejected a Clark poem; both she and her mother, Camille Yuill, were good friends with the poet. Poems from the *Chronicle* were published as *Sky Lines and Wood Smoke* in 1935. After Clark's death, Jessie published *boots and bylines,* including poems and letters from his later life which had appeared in the newspaper during his lifetime, but had not been included in *Sky Lines and Wood Smoke*. Jessie subsequently became my friend and mentor, and partly as a result of her work, Badger Clark was such a part of my growing up that I've always felt as if he were a relative, perhaps a kindly uncle.

To memorize Clark's poems, I practiced reciting them while moving cows to pasture. I'd read a particular poem two or three times before starting the ride, then try to recall it as my horse clip-clopped behind the cattle. The poetic rhythms often fit perfectly with the movement of the horse, and feeling that rhythm could sometimes help me find the line I was searching for in my brain. On days when the cows were slow, my father probably heard me bawling, "At a roundup on the Gily one sweet morning long ago" to make them move.

Decades later, I discovered and attended the National Cowboy Poetry Gathering in Elko, NV, where many people recite poetry to the beat of a horse's hooves. I was able to read and recite my own poetry as well as Badger's. And another time, I was waiting my turn to recite in front of a crowd in New York City when the great cowboy poet Paul Zarzyski momentarily froze while reciting Badger's popular "The Legend of Boastful Bill." Knowing just how he felt, I was proud to be able to bellow the line to him.

During high school, I regularly recited Badger's poems in declamation contests; my favorite, which I discovered still lurking in my brain and was able to recite without rehearsal at the gathering in Elko a few years ago, might be "The Westerner."

> *My fathers sleep on the sunrise plains*
> *and each one sleeps alone.*
> *Their trails may dim to the grass and rains,*
> *For I choose to make my own.*

Mumbling this poem under my breath at key points in my life

has helped me make my own trail.

Another of my favorites is "The Plainsmen:"

> *Men of the older, gentler soil,*
> *Loving the things that their fathers wrought—*

Yet another is "From Town," which like most of the poems in my copy of *Sun and Saddle Leather* is filled with notations about how to recite a particular word or line:

> *We're the children of the open and we hate the haunts of men.*
>
> *But we had to come to town to get the mail. . . . .*
>
> *We acquired our hasty temper from our friend, the centipede.*

My note beside this stanza reads "Boastfully."

> *From the rattlesnake we learnt to guard our rights.*
>
> *We have gathered fightin' pointers from the famous bronco steed*
>
> *And the bobcat teached us reppertee that bites.*

Of course, his most popular and best-known poem, "The Cowboy's Prayer," is often reproduced on placemats, t-shirts, mugs, and funeral programs as having been written by "anonymous." (I received a "Superior" rating for reciting it at the State Declamation Contest in 1959.) The false attribution happened even during Clark's lifetime; eventually he grew philosophical about what was outright ignorance or overt plagiarism.

Why did I write letters to Badger Clark? I wasn't merely writing as a fan. In 1957, the seventh and eighth grade students of Hermosa Grade School, under the direction of Mrs. Anna Tubbs, put together a historical project. We interviewed older residents of the communities around Hermosa, recorded their stories, and made a scrapbook. We dedicated that scrapbook to Badger Clark, and made plans for the class to visit him at The Badger Hole. (I hope the scrapbook is right where we placed it when our project was finished: at the Custer County 1881 Courthouse Museum.)

Badger Clark's response to my first letter was postmarked Custer, S.D., Feb. 7, 1957, 2 p.m., and typed on a manual typewriter on paper with a simple letterhead:

Badger Clark

Custer South Dakota

9 February, 1957

Dear Linda,

> Thank you very much for the honors you confer upon me by dedicating your scrapbook to me. It is hard for me to realize that I am becoming an old-timer, though not a pioneer. For so many years I have looked to older men as old-timers but now, all of a sudden, those men are gone and there seems to be nobody left but men younger than I. It is a strange feeling and someday, a long way ahead, I hope, you will experience it.
>
> As I have written Mrs. Tubbs, I have no speaking engagements this spring and you are free to set your own date, but, as I told her, with a big crowd and a small cabin, it might be well to put it in April or May when, with good luck the weather will be warm enough for the

party to spread out on the porch. I've entertained as many as twenty-five young people here in the house, but that's about the limit. If you want to have a lunch and roast wieners, I have both a range and a fireplace.

Last, I want to congratulate you on being able to express yourself on paper. Writing and reading are both neglected arts in these days. The other day I heard of an eighth-grade boy, writing some sort of an exercise for school, who had to ask his mother how to spell "catch." And every now and then I get a letter from a college graduate which contains misspelled words or bad grammar, or both. It is a pleasure to get a letter like yours.

Good Luck.

Badger Clark

My head swelled immodestly at his praise, and I solemnly showed the letter to my parents, who were sticklers for grammatical expression. I'm sure they felt proud that their training was having an effect on me, and surely this praise had something to do with my continuing the writing I'd already begun.

Badger's second communication to me is a 2-cent postcard postmarked

2 p.m. April 26, 1957.
Badger Hole, 25 April.
Dear Linda:

I shall be away for nine or ten days during the first half of May and in fact it is hard for me to know just what days I shall be at home during the month. This is my busy season, you know—commencements and the like, and I expect the last month of school will bring various special occasions for you. As it is so late, I believe we had better postpone our party until after school begins in the fall. The weather will be more dependable then, for one thing. That may look like a long time to you, but when you're my age, you'll know it ain't, it ain't, it ain't!

Badger Clark died that fall, September 26, 1957, at age 74, before he could visit us. I am 75 years old.

Recently I was asked to record some of my thoughts about Hermosa history for the Hermosa Arts and History Association and realized with a shock that I am now one of the older residents still able to do so. Just as Badger predicted, I am now one of the old-timers and while the date of these events may seem recent to me, "it ain't, it ain't, it ain't!"

In 2009, I was asked to write about "poetry in daily life" for the National Cowboy Poetry Gathering (Elko, NV), program. Naturally, I turned to Badger Clark for inspiration, and this is what I wrote:

One sweet mornin' long ago, my Arabian mare and I were trailing cows and calves home from summer pasture near the Badlands, where *the sharp crests dream in the sunset gleam.*

My father's green '49 Chevy pickup idled in front; Rebel nipped slow cows on the tail, and I day-dreamed about riding wilder horses after faster cows while reciting lines from Badger Clark's poetry.

> *I kin ride the highest liver*

> *'Tween the Gulf and Powder River*

For my twelfth birthday, I'd gotten *Sun and Saddle Leather* by Badger Clark, South Dakota's poet laureate and one of the finest cowboy poets ever. I began to hear *The Legend of Boastful Bill* in my head.

> *So Bill climbed the Northern Fury*
> *And they mangled up the air*

While I recited, Rebel twitched an ear, jingling her bridle to the hoofbeat rhythm. By the time the cows ambled home, I'd recalled most of the words. My father didn't care for Bill's methods:

> *I'll cinch 'im up and spur 'im till he's broke*

but he could recite most of *The Rime of the Ancient Mariner* and *Snowbound*. Mother preferred ballads:

> *Summer of 'sixty-three, sir, and Conrad*
> *was gone away--*
> *Gone to the country town, sir,*
> *to sell our first load of hay.*

She'd learned *Kentucky Belle* in grade school. When she was 91, we recited it together, tears in our eyes, reminiscing about the past, or, as Badger put it:

> *Men of the older, gentler soil*

Poetry is part of everyone's daily life. The advertising jingle you can't get out of your head is someone's best effort at making you remember. If you remember a phrase for a long time, it's likely to be poetic.

For example, after 25 years, I can still see the blonde driving the pickup with this poetic bumper sticker:

You've never lived

until you've loved a sheepherder

Samuel Taylor Coleridge called poetry "the best words in the best order." Making a living as an itinerant writer, I drive a lot, remembering good lines to force the ads and bad jokes out of my brain. Many of the lines that return to my mind again and again are Badger Clark's.

Over the Springtime plains I ride,

Knee to knee with Spring

Poetry romps me through bleak regions with bad radio stations, keeps me from tuneless singing. With poets as passengers, I'm never alone. Badger reminds me:

I stand here, where the bright skies blaze

over me and the big today.

A day that starts with poetry is better than one without. Online, I often read www.cowboypoetry.com and *The Writer's Almanac*. I hate going to town, but when I do, I warble:

For we found that city life is a constant round of strife

And we ain't the breed for shyin' from a fray.

Badger lived just up the road from me, about thirty miles away in Custer State Park. His modest cabin is now a tourist destination of a quiet nature. Passing the turnoff to the park on my way to get the mail at the post office in Hermosa, I picture him in his cabin, reciting some of my favorite verses:

And we're ridin' home at daybreak–'cause the air is cooler then–

All 'cept one of us that stopped behind in jail.
Letters piled on the seat, I hurry home to my real work, declaiming as he did on the plight of every writer:

Just a-writin', a-writin',
Nothin' I like half so well
As a-slingin' ink and English–
if the stuff will only sell."
Linda M. Hasselstrom, Windbreak House, 2009

Quotations in the preceding essay are from the following sources:

One sweet mornin' long ago,
—from *The Legend of Boastful Bill*

the sharp crests dream in the sunset gleam.
—from *The Bad Lands*

I kin ride the highest liver
'Tween the Gulf and Powder River
So Bill climbed the Northern Fury
And they mangled up the air
I'll cinch 'im up and spur 'im till he's broke
–all from *The Legend of Boastful Bill.*

"Kentucky Belle" was written by Constance Fenimore Woolson.

Men of the older, gentler soil
—from *The Plainsmen*

When Hot Springs Was A Pup

> *Over the Springtime plains I ride,*
> *Knee to knee with Spring*

–from *The Springtime Plains*

> *I stand here, where the bright skies blaze*
> *over me and the big today.*

From *The Westerner*

> *We're the children of the open and we hate the haunts o'men,*
> *But we had to come to town to get the mail.*
> *And we're ridin' home at daybreak—'cause the air is cooler then—*
> *All 'cept one of us that stopped behind in jail*

—both from *From Town*

> *"Just a-writin', a-writin',*
> *Nothin' I like half so well*
> *As a-slingin' ink and English—*
> *if the stuff will only sell."*

This is part of a two-verse poem inscribed by Badger Clark on a copy of *Sun and Saddle Leather*, and quoted in the Preface to the 1952 edition, written by "R.H.," Ruth Hill, an editor at Chapman and Grimes.

Afterword: A Cowboy's Prayer

Peggy A. Sanders

In South Dakota and other middle-of-the-country states' rural schools there was a student organization called Y.C.L.—Young Citizens League. Through it we learned how to conduct meetings following Robert's Rules of Order, the etiquette of putting up and taking down the outdoor American flag and folding it correctly. We held practice elections for president, learning civics by doing—all with the intent of teaching citizenship.

One of the Y.C.L events in which all of Fall River County's rural school students participated was an annual Music Festival. Students learned selected songs in advance and these renditions were performed as a group chorus. One year a poem, *A Roundup Lullaby* that Badger Clark wrote and had been set to music by J.E. "Aim" Morhardt, was a chosen song. It was my musical introduction to Badger. The words are so memorable that I can still recall the lyrics all of these years later. The first verse goes like this:

> *Desert blue and silver in the still moonshine,*
> *Coyotes lapping lazy on the hill.*
> *Sleepy wings of lightnin' down the far skyline,*
> *Time for millin' cattle to be still."*

The words paint an illustration as graphic as a photo, particularly for anyone who has been around coyotes and cattle.

Lest anyone think Badger was provincial, perhaps because he

lived as a bachelor in a cabin he built in the woods, he was a solitary figure by choice. He was in demand as a speaker and traveled throughout the US as much as he desired. Badger worked independently and also spent time with the Redpath Chautauqua circuit. He would come home to replenish himself and to write poetry in the quiet. In a letter to Ralph Shearer, a Methodist minister and personal friend, Badger wrote on June 13, 1934. "For twelve years, nearly a quarter of my life, I have lived alone, and it suits me so well that when I go off on a trip though people are kind to me and do everything they can to make me comfortable, I soon get fidgety and wistful and homesick for this little shack."

Living on WG Flat, I can relate.

Badger Clark died before I was six years old and I never got to meet him nor hear him speak. Yet when I see photos of him in his tall boots and distinguished hats, and listen to a recording of him reciting this poem, it is almost as if I was there when he spoke at local graduations and Y.C.L. events. This poem, my favorite of Badger's, is often attributed to "anonymous."

A Cowboy's Prayer
Badger Clark

Oh, Lord, I've never lived where churches grow.
I love creation better as it stood
That day you finished it so long ago.
And looked upon Your work and called it good.
I know that others find You in the light
That's sifted down through tinted window panes,

And yet I seem to feel You near tonight
In this dim, quiet starlight on the plains.
I thank you, Lord, that I am placed so well,
That you have made my freedom so complete;
That I'm no slave to whistle, clock or bell,
Nor weak-eyed prisoner of wall and street.
Just let me live my life as I've begun
And give me work that's open to the sky;
Make me a partner of the wind and sun,
And I won't ask a life that's soft or high.
Let me be easy on the man that's down;
Let me be square and generous with all.
I'm careless sometimes, Lord, when I'm in town,
 But never let them say I'm mean or small!
Make me as big and open as the plains,
As honest as the hawse between my knees,
Clean as the wind that blows behind the rains,
Free as the hawk that circles down the breeze.
Forgive me, Lord, if sometimes I forget.
You know about the reasons that are hid.
You understand the things that gall and fret;
You know me better than my mother did.
Just keep an eye on all that's done and said
 And right me, sometimes, when I turn aside,
And guide me on the long, dim trail ahead
That stretches upward toward the Great Divide.

Charles Badger Clark, Jr. (Badger Clark) chronology

1883, January 1: born in Albia, Iowa to Charles Badger Clark, Sr. and Mary Ellen (Cleaver) Clark

1883, spring: family moved to Plankinton, SD, later to Mitchell, SD, then Huron, SD

1894: Badger's brother, Frederick, died of tuberculosis

1898, April: family moved to Deadwood, mother died from TB on October 7

1901, June 20: father married Anna Morris, schoolteacher and talented amateur poet. Deadwood residence was at 41 Forest Ave.

1902: graduated from Deadwood High School

1902-1903: attended Dakota Wesleyan University for one year

1903, December 18: arrived in Cuba with group of 30, intending to colonize; led by E. D. Kerr of Mitchell, SD

1905: returned to Deadwood; first engagement to Helen Fowler

1905: summer surveyor in the SD Badlands, then reporter for Lead *Daily Call*

1906, April: Badger moved to Arizona to help his tuberculosis

1906, August: *Pacific Monthly* published Badger's first paid poetry; originally titled "Arizony," later titled "Ridin' "

1906, December: "A Cowboy's Prayer," was first published in *Pacific Monthly*

1907: Reverend C.B. Clark named first chaplain at Battle Mountain Sanitarium in Hot Springs

1910: returned to South Dakota; started going by Badger Clark instead of C.B. Clark, Jr.

This house at 538 Jennings Avenue, previously 705 8th Street, in Hot Springs was the home of Reverend C.B. and Anna Morris Clark. Badger spent several years there while he helped take care of his ailing father.

Peggy Sanders photo

1910-1925: lived with his parents at 705 8th St. in Hot Springs to help take care of his ailing father and assist Anna.

1911: second engagement to Helen Fowler, broke up and abandoned marriage plans later that year

1911: mid-year, *Pacific Monthly* acquired by *Sunset Magazine* which continued to publish Badger's work

1915: published his first book of poetry, *Sun and Saddle Leather* which begins with "Ridin'"

1915: his first official public speech was given at South Dakota State University.

1916: until his health failed in 1957, Badger spoke across the nation from New York to California

1917: published poetry book called *Grass Grown Trails*

1917, November 16: walked 62 miles to Rapid City in 17 hours, just for fun

1920, March: *Ladies Home Journal* published his first fiction piece, "A Great Institution," later included in *Spike*

1921: father died

1921-24: traveled with Redpath Chautauqua group

1924: Anna moved into the SD State Soldiers' Home in Hot Springs

1925: Badger moved to Custer State Park, lived in cabin owned by the state

1925: published *Spike*, a book of funny stories about his life in Arizona

1927, December: Badger was named the first Poet Laureate of South Dakota

1927: Hot Springs Kiwanis Club published Badger's *When Hot Springs Was a Pup*

1932: started laying foundation for his own cabin, The Badger Hole, which he constructed with a little help

This photo of Badger is from his days at the house on Jennings Avenue.

Dakota Wesleyan University Archives, McGovern Library, Dakota Wesleyan University, Mitchell, South Dakota.

1933, March 30 through June 30, 1942: popular speaker at area Civilian Conservation Corps camps

1935: published *Sky Lines and Wood Smoke*

1937: Anna Morris Clark died

1937: used his inheritance to finish The Badger Hole, his private cabin in Custer State Park, lived there 20 years

1957 September 26: died of lung cancer; buried at Evergreen Cemetery, Hot Springs

Additional Reading and Resources

Books by Charles Badger Clark

Grass-Grown Trails. Boston: Richard G. Badger, 1917 (see *Sun and Saddle Leather*)

Sun and Saddle Leather. (Includes *Grass Grown Trails* and new poems) Boston: Chapman & Grimes, 1919

This was the first collection of Badger Clark poems to be published, in 1915, and remains his most popular book. Extolling the cowboy life of the Old West in general and of Arizona Territory in particular, it was later combined with his second volume of southwestern poems, *Grass Grown Trails* (1917). Since 1920 that edition has never been out of print. Included are many words and phrases in Spanish, a language which he first picked up during a year and a half spent in Cuba.

Spike. Boston, Mass: Richard D. Badger, The Gorham Press, 1925

Autobiographical fiction; stories taken from letters to his stepmother, revised, fictionalized. Badger Clark's only collection of prose fiction, *Spike* was originally published in 1925, bringing together many of his previously published short stories said to be based on the life of his ranch foreman in Arizona Territory. Badger's instinct for storytelling shines in these humorous short stories, replete with dialect and cowboy wisdom.

When Hot Springs Was a Pup. Hot Springs, SD: Kiwanis Club, 1927. Lame Johnny Press, Hermosa, SD, 1976, 1983. Badger

Clark Memorial Society, Fenske Media Corporation, Rapid City, SD 2011.

This is the only book the cowboy poet wrote on assignment and was published as tourism promotional piece. It includes the forward by long-time Hot Springs resident Kennett Harris. This volume showcases the author's innate humor and storytelling skills.

Sky Lines and Wood Smoke. Custer, SD: The Chronicle Shop, 1935

With his return to the Black Hills, Badger began to write more about his home state of South Dakota, exploring themes of nature, faith and patriotism from a western perspective. The author's pride in his home state and the people who inhabited it are evident in this collection of new and previously published poems from the Custer County Chronicle.

boots and bylines. Custer, SD: Jessie Y. Sundstrom, Hartman Printing, 1978

Posthumous; poems and letters from the files of the *Custer County Chronicle*; comments by Camille Yuill. Published after Badger Clark's death, *boots and bylines* includes poems and letters from Badger Clark's later life which appeared in the newspaper during his lifetime, but had not been included in *Sky Lines and Woodsmoke*. They provide a window into the times and activities of his last twenty years.

Badger Clark, Cowboy Poet with Universal Appeal. Custer, SD: Jessie Y. Sundstrom, 1978.

First published in paperback, this book was expanded and reprinted in 2004, including more photographs and details of the poet laureate's personal life, along with three poems. Written by historian and publisher, Jessie Y. Sundstrom in her capacity as Executive Director of the Badger Clark Memorial Society, this biography includes an extensive bibliography. (The Badger Clark Memorial Society no longer exists.)

God of the Open. Black Hills United Methodist Historical Society, Nauman Printing, Inc., 1981. Includes biography and several poems.

A History of Custer State Park. Pamphlet, Custer State Park, n.d.; reprinted by Badger Clark Memorial Society, 1994.

Custer State Park: Black Hills of South Dakota. Badger Clark. n.d. Reprinted on the 75th anniversary of Custer State Park and the tenth anniversary of The Badger Clark Memorial Society, 1994.

Other sources:

The Literature of South Dakota. Coursey, O. W. Mitchell, SD: Educator Supply Co., 1923. Includes photo, biography and several poems.

The Badger Clark Story. Morganti, Helen F. No city or publisher; November 1, 1960. Printed by Espe Printing Company, 31 East Omaha, Rapid City, South Dakota. First Edition.

Morganti was the first woman public relations director for the Black Hills Ordnance Depot at Igloo, SD and the Sioux Ordnance Depot at Sidney, NE while she served in the U.S. Army Corps of Engineers. Over the years she taught in Edgemont High School, Lead High School and Black Hills

State College. She was a member of numerous press and women's organization and the American Legion.

Her book is a biography, and includes bibliography of references to and by Badger Clark.

Papers belonging to Jessie Sundstrom and Camille Yuill, both of whom were close friends with Badger Clark, have been catalogued at the Homestake Adams Archives and Research Center in Deadwood.

The Helen Magee Collection in the Hot Springs, SD Public Library has material on and by Badger Clark. *hotspringspubliclibrary.com*

Badger Clark materials in the archives at the McGovern Library, Dakota Wesleyan University, Mitchell, SD include a scrapbook Badger assembled that contained accounts of his time in Cuba and Arizona, letters to his family from both places, and numerous photographs.

The South Dakota Historical Society Foundation, SDHSF.org lists a collection of six hardback books in a display box as *The Collected Works of Badger Clark,* including

>*boots and bylines*
>
>*Sky Lines and Wood Smoke*
>
>*Spike*
>
>*Sun and Saddle Leather*
>
>*When Hot Springs was a Pup,* and
>
>*Badger Clark, Cowboy Poet with Universal Appeal* by Jessie Sundstrom

Additional resources:

Badger Clark Ballads, Musical scores by J.E. "Aim" Morhardt,, 1982. Westerners International, Tucson, AZ.

Twenty-three of Badger's poems, including "A Border Affair" a.k.a. "Spanish Is the Loving Tongue" and "A Cowboy's Prayer" were set to musical scores.

An Annotated Bibliography of the Works of Badger Clark, Cowboy Poet. 1987. Shebby Lee. Westerners International, Tucson, AZ.

Cowboy Poetry: Classic Poems & Prose by Badger Clark. Greg Scott, ed. Phoenix, AZ: Cowboy Miner Productions, 2005.

Poetry, photos, short stories, and essays by Badger Clark with biographical information, notes on poems and stories and a photo album. Includes short stories and poems which had never been reprinted.

Badger Clark: Dakota Voices, CD no city nor publisher given. Story and poems read by Badger Clark and others. The first seven out of the 26 recordings on this CD are the actual voice of Badger Clark, who died in 1957. His final recording is a speech excerpt delivered at a Dakota Wesleyan University picnic, date and location unknown. Although the speech is incomplete, it is included to show Badger Clark's sense of humor, natural exuberance, and disdain for hypocrisy. Although lecturing was his main source of income for over thirty years, this is the only known recording of a formal speech by the cowboy poet.

Mountain Thunder: The Ballad of Badger Clark, Kenn Pierson, Pine Hill Press, Freeman, SD, 1993.

Theater play script in book form.

Mountain Thunder: A Ballad of Badger Clark

DVD. *Mountain Thunder: A Ballad of Badger Clark* is the dramatic portrayal of Badger Clark, South Dakota's first poet laureate. The drama, based on the play of the same title by Kenn Pierson, illustrates the personality, philosophy and essence of Badger Clark, the "cowboy poet," through a dramatic monologue in which the poet reacts to letters from a friend. Darryl F. Patten, former Director of Drama at Dakota Wesleyan University, Mitchell, South Dakota, stars as Badger Clark.

The Music of Badger Clark. The Badger Sett Band. CDBaby.com. 2013.

The Music of Badger Clark, Volume ll. Pegie Douglas & The Badger Sett Band. CDBaby.com. 2018.

Pegie Douglas, a resident of the Black Hills, has put several of Badger's poems to her original music. She is a regular performer in the Black Hills and other venues. The band name comes from this fact: a badger hole is called a badger sett, particularly in England. pegiedouglas.com

The Badger Hole in Custer State Park. This pamphlet was written for Custer State Park as a guide to The Badger Hole, Clark's log cabin in the park, including some biographical details, photographs and poems.

Cowboypoetry.com includes considerable information about Badger Clark, including some of his poetry, an introduction to the 1922 edition of *Sun and Saddle Leather,* information about recordings of cowboy poets reciting Badger's work and musicians who have set it to music, and much, much more. The site even includes a report on the first annual workshop Linda M. Hasselstrom taught in his honor in 2006, with photos of The Badger Hole, and information on the movie about him, *Mountain Thunder*.

Editor's note: Neither Badger Clark nor his many supporters paid much attention to copyright law or the requirements of legitimate publication, so various editions of many of his works appear without copyright notice, or without information about the publishers. Some of these editions appear to be facsimiles produced by British publishers who freely admit that they may include typographical and other errors. And numerous contradictions occur in the various sources, even though several knew Badger Clark personally, indicating that someone's memory may have been faulty. We'd welcome definitive information on any discrepancies.

Beware: A 2018 search online for books by Charles Badger Clark showed, along with some books he actually wrote, titles like *Cow-country Killer, Pawnee Dawn, Round Mountain Range, Secret Mesa,* and *Singleton*, all published between 1976 and 1977. These books were all written by Lauran Bosworth Paine (born Lawrence Kerfman Duby Jr.), who wrote hundreds of Westerns, romance, science fiction and mystery novels. *Singleton* (London: Robert Hale, 1978) is listed by some legitimate sources as a Badger Clark book, but Wikipedia.com notes that Lauran Bosworth Paine was the author, "writing as Badger Clark."

Biographies of the Editors

Linda M. Hasselstrom's published writing includes 17 books of nonfiction and poetry, including most recently *Write Now, Here's How* (2020), *Gathering from the Grassland: A Plains Journal,* (2017) *Dakota: Bones, Grass, Sky: Collected and New Poems* (2017), and *The Wheel of the Year: A Writer's Workbook,* (2015). *Dirt Songs: A Plains Duet* with Nebraska State Poet Twyla Hansen (Backwaters Press) received the 2012 Nebraska Book Award for Poetry. Hasselstrom has received recognition for Distinguished Service to the Humanities from the South Dakota Humanities Council and is special consultant to the Rural Lit RALLY initiative, State University of New York, Buffalo, NY. Among her memberships are The Author's Guild, Inc., Western Folklife Center, Elko, NV and Women Writing the West. She holds an M.A. degree from the University of Missouri-Columbia. Her western South Dakota ranch hosts the Great Plains Native Plant Society's botanic garden for grassland plants, and she conducts writing retreats in person and by email at her Windbreak House Retreat; she has worked with more than 300 writers from 31 states. *Windbreakhouse.com Facebook.com/WindbreakHouse*.

Peggy A. Sanders is a follower of local history whose great-grandparents Ira and Hattie Tillotson homesteaded near Cascade, Dakota Territory in 1883; six generations of their descendants have lived and worked in Fall River County, always in agriculture. She has written five Images of America books including *Fall River County and Hot Springs: 125 Years; The Civilian Conservation Corps in and Around the Black Hills; Custer County (SD); Wind Cave National Park: The First 100 Years, and Fall River County and Hot Springs: Views from the Past 1881-1955*. She is a contributor to the anthologies, *Woven on the Wind* and *Life on the Farm and Ranch: South Dakota Stories*. She is a member of Western Writers of America and Wyoming Writers, Inc. Sanders serves on the SD State Historical Society Board of Trustees.

She is the originator and past chairman of the Focus on Fall River County History Conference, held annually in Hot Springs, SD. She is on the Board of Directors of the Civilian Conservation Corps Museum in Hill City, SD, a museum she helped create. A columnist since 1999, Sanders won the National Society of Newspaper Columnists' Will Rogers Writing Contest in 2007. Sanders earned her B.A. from Central College, Pella, IA after spending her junior year at the Sorbonne, Paris, France. *www.peggysanders.com*

Photographers

Whenever known, the photographers have been credited for their work and acknowledgements are in order.

Stevens Studio was established during 1912 in Hot Springs, SD, by H.B. (Herman) Stevens when he and his wife, Evangel Livingston Stevens relocated from Omaha. In 1946 Stevens sold to James H. (Jimmy) Snyder and Maurice (Ozzie) Osman. Three years later Osman bought Snyder out when he re-enlisted in the Army. Ozzie and his wife Ruth ran the studio under the Stevens Studio name until 1986, providing 74 years of photo history in and around Fall River County, SD. The Pioneer Museum collection is the largest repository of Stevens Studio work, including photos from 1912.

H.B. (Herman) and his wife, Evangel Livingston Stevens, opened Stevens Studio in 1912.

Jimmy Snyder was a partner in Stevens Studio from 1946 to 1949.

Ruth and Ozzie Osman ran Stevens Studio for 40 years.

The photos credited to Horan Collection were digitally sent to the museum by Barb Horan who lives in New Jersey. Her great-grandfather, Robert Quayle, was superintendent of the Chicago Northwestern Railway. As a result, he had the opportunity to take trips on luxurious railroad cars from his home in Chicago to the Black Hills for vacation and/or business or both. The photos Horan sent include the 1903 fire that burned the wooden buildings for nearly a block; they were replaced by the sandstone Minnekahta Block and additional stone buildings after the fire.

In 1903 Robert and Clara Quayle, pictured here, came to Hot Springs on a C & N Railway private luxury car. The photographer is unknown but likely was an employee of the railroad.

Horan Collection

W.R. (William Richard) Cross was a photographer in Hot Springs, SD from 1880-1907. During those same years he plied his trade at Ft. Abraham Lincoln, and at Ft. Meade.

From *They Captured the Moment: Dakotas Photographers 1853-1920* by Robert Kolbe with Brian Bade.

This self-portrait shows John C. H. Grabill, a photographer based in Deadwood, Lead, Rockerville and Sturgis from 1885-1891. During 1891-1893, he was at Hot Springs and Deadwood under the company name Grabill Portrait & View Company.

From *They Captured the Moment: Dakotas Photographers 1853-1920* by Robert Kolbe with Brian Bade.

Arundel C. Hull, pioneer photographer, took some of the first photos along the Union Pacific Railroad during the summers of 1867 and 1868. In 1869 he accompanied William H. Jackson to Utah and remained there after Jackson returned to Omaha on September 27. Hull worked to fulfill the photo contract with the railroad. On January 1, 1870, Hull established a permanent studio in Fremont, Nebraska. Jackson later acknowledged that many of the photos in the Union Pacific collection were taken by Hull, although Jackson got the credit. Hull traveled widely which included a foray to Hot Springs, SD, and he took a treasure trove of early Hot Springs photos. From *Photographer of the Early West: The Story of Arundel Hull* by Eugene A. Miller

Frank Jay Haynes started his photography studio in Fargo, Dakota Territory during 1878. He became a photographer for the Northern Pacific Railroad and traveled while taking photos from the company until 1905. He is primarily known for his extensive photo work in Yellowstone National Park from 1884 to 1921.

Photograph & Illustration Index

Dedication
Introduction
    Dragoon Mountains, Arizona xv

Requiem for a Cowboy Poet
    Young Badger Clark, 1908 xix
    Badger Clark in his study xxiii
    The Badger Hole xxv
    Rocky Canyon 1

Red Rocks and Red Men
    Water analysis table 4
    Rocks in the river channel 6
    Buffalo Gap 8
    Battle Mountain 9
    Sioux Indian Chiefs 11

Tepee to Log Cabin
    Wagon train 14
    Tepee ring 15
    Parkman, Francis 16
    Ross, H. N. 17
    Thornby, W. J. 18
    Fall River Falls 19
    Minnekahta Avenue 21
    Trimmer house 22
    Trimmer, G. M. 23
    Dennis, John 24
    Evans, Fred T. 25

Stewart, Alexander S. 26

Jennings, R. D. 27

Moses, Sam 28

Point of Rocks 29

Stewart, Alexander house 30

Red Cloud 31

Travois 33

Peirce, Doc 34

More Firsts

Wind Cave 35

Bingham, Tom 36

Dennis, John house 37

Gibson Hotel 37

Stewart, A. S. residence (1891) 38

Stagecoach 39

Jensen, Chris 40

Sisters' Hospital 41

Minnekahta panorama 42

Brick store at Oelrichs 43

Eastman, C. S. 44

Sheperd, James 45

Martin Valley Ranch 47

Martin, E. W. 48

Cowboys and Ladies

Bar T Ranch 50

Bar T Brand 51

Bar Oarlock Brand 51

Ranch location map 52

Blanketed Indian woman 53
Jennings, Mattie Mrs. 54
Pierce, Fred cowboy 55
13th Calvary 57
3rd Infantry 57
Cowboys 58
Evans, Theresa 60
Bingham, Matt 61
Zither 62
Lincoln Hall 63
Tillotson, Claude 65
Stanley, Ward 67
Marty, George 67
Supper at open range 68

The Pup Gets Its Eyes Opened

Grubbs, W. T. 70
Bull team 73
Minnekahta Hotel 76
Hot Springs Star office 77
Hot Springs Star masthead 78
Tourism booklet 79
Tallyho Coach 80
Evans Hotel, train 81

Religion, Law and Literature

Chautauqua church service 84
Catholic church 85
Methodist church 86
Eureka 88

Temperance ribbon	89
Cowboys, bedrolls, wagon	90
Man in Fall River	92
Marty, Joe	95
Wilson Law office	96
Riding Sidesaddle	98
Hesperian	99

Boom!

State Soldiers' Home	102
Evans Quarry	103
Fargo-Dickover Building	104
Evans, Fred freighting	104
Hot Springs House	105
Evans Plunge, horses & buggies	106
Evans Plunge, 1890 postcard	107
Gillespie Hotel under construction	108
Black Hills College	109
Hot Springs High School	109
Presbyterian Church	110
Chautauqua	111
Fire, 1903	113
Minnekahta Block	114
Miles, Nelson General, and staff	116
Pine Ridge Indian Camp	117
Wyatt, William	119

The End of the Trail

Courthouse	121
Canyon buggy ride	124

Train cars, Northwestern 125
Union Depot 126
Evans Hotel 127
Nichols Sanitarium 128
Catholicon 130
Siloam Bathhouse 130
Battle Mountain Sanitarium... 131
Trees on North River Street 133
Coolidge/Battle Mountain Sanitarium 133
Bridge on 7th Street 134
Coolidge and group 135
Coolidge at SD State Soldiers' Home 136

Hot Springs Characters
Editors' notes on the text
Afterword: Slingin' Ink and English
Afterword: A Cowboy's Prayer
Charles Badger Clark, Jr. (Badger Clark) chronology

Clark home 163
Badger on banister with guitar 165

Additional Reading and Resources
Biographies of the Editors
Photographers

H. B. Herman 176
Jimmy Snyder 177
Ruth & Ozzie Osman 177
Robert & Clara Quayle 178
Cross, W. R. 179

Grabill, C. H. Self portrait 179

Hull, Arundel C. 180

Haynes, Frank Jay 181

Index

Points of Interest

Map with points of interest marked 197

USGS Map of Hot Springs 1984 198

Front Cover

Bathing, Hot Springs, S.D.

Back Cover

Badger Clark

Index

A

Anglo-American Cattle Company ... 43
Arikara ... 5

B

Badger Hole ... xxii–xxvi, 152–153, 164, 166, 172–173
Baptist ... 111
Bar Oarlock ranch ... 95. *See also* Oar Lock Ranch
Bar T Ranch ... 28, 50
Battle Mountain ... 11, 12, 36, 72, 80, 96, 101, 137, 138
Battle Mountain Sanitarium ... xxi, xxiv, 9, 129, 131, 134, 142, 147, 163
Bell, Jim ... 50
Belle Fourche ... 16
Berrier, Elizabeth ... 99
Bingham, Matt ... 61, 64, 137
Bingham, Tom ... 35, 36
Black Hills College ... 108–110
Black Hills of South Dakota ... 15, 169
Black Mountains ... 1
Bodega Bar ... 88
Brundschmidt, Joe ... 22
Buffalo Gap, South Dakota ... 7, 22, 29, 31, 69, 72, 80, 101, 121, 134, 141, 143, 144
Burke Quarry ... 102
Burlington & Missouri River Railroad ... 101, 121, 124, 125, 147

C

California ... 17, 164
Callahan, Frank ... 46
Catholicon Bathhouse/hotel ... 130
Catholicon Peak ... 23
Catholic parish house ... 62
Chautauqua ... xxv, 111–112, 160, 164
Cheyenne Indians ... 7–11, 136
Cheyenne River ... 50, 61, 82, 93, 118–119, 147
Cheyenne River Bridge ... 22
Clark, Dave ... 52
Clark, Phil ... 50
Commercial Gazette of Cincinnati ... 82
Connor, R. F. ... 112
Coolidge, President and Mrs. (Calvin, Grace) ... 133–137
Country Club ... 136
Crane, Mrs. Jay (Elizabeth) ... 99

Crane, William ... 112
Crawford, Nebraska ... 56–57
Cross, William Richard, Photographer ... xii, 179
Custer County ... 42, 44, 146, 152
Custer, South Dakota ... 15, 25, 39, 141, 143, 152

D

Dakota Hot Springs Company ... 72
Davidson, John ... 20
Deadwood Coach ... 38, 39
Deadwood, South Dakota ... xvi, xviii, 15, 28, 30, 38, 48, 59, 69, 72–74, 80, 105, 140–142, 144, 162, 170
Denman, J. L. ... 48
Dennis, John ... 23, 24, 37
Dennis, Miss Mattie ... 24
Dickover, J. B. ... 112
Donohue, Cornelius (Lame Johnny) ... 34
Dr. Jennings ... 55
Dr. Stewart ... 63
Dry Creek ... 52
Dudley, Hon. E. G., Judge ... 63, 72, 74, 96, 105

E

Eastman, Charles Sumner (Charlie) ... 44, 96, 122–123, 144–145
Eastman, Dean ... 96
Eastman, Mrs. Charles ... 123
Eaton, Major Henry Z. ... 63
Edgemont, South Dakota ... 121, 169
Eighth Street ... xxi, 61, 136, 139
Elkhorn Railroad ... 101
Eureka Bar ... 88
Evans, F. (Fred) Sr. ... 9, 25, 72–74, 101, 104–105, 111, 114, 126–127, 140
Evans, Mrs. Fred (Theresa M.) ... 59–60
Evans Heights, Hot Springs ... 36
Evans Hotel ... 81, 127
Evans Plunge ... 106, 147
Evans Quarry ... 103, 114

F

Falling Water River ... 81
Fall River County ... vii, 42–44, 47, 142, 146, 159, 175, 176
Fall River County courthouse ... 96
Fall River Falls ... 19

Fall River Road ... 92, 103, 114, 124
Fargo-Dickover Building ... 104
Ferguson, Orlando ... 130
Flatiron Building ... 37
Flying V Ranch ... 51–52, 71
Fort Meade ... 57
Fort Robinson ... 57
Fremont, Elkhorn & Missouri Valley Railroad ... 69, 81
French Creek ... 13, 18, 52

G

Gardner, Captain C. V. ... 143
Germond, W.J. (Bill) ... 22
Ghost Dance ... 115
Gibson Hotel ... 37
Gillespie, F. D. ... 112
Gillespie Hotel ... 21, 81, 107, 108
Goddard, Lon ... 52
Grabill, John C., Photographer ... 179
Graves, L. R. ... 72, 74
Great Lakes ... 7
Louie Green ... 52

H

Happy Hollow ... 110–111
Hargens, Dr. C. W. ... 144
Harris, Kennett ... vi, 97, 100, 144, 168
The Hatchet ... 97–98
Hat Creek ... 50
Helgerson, Mrs., first school teacher ... 36
Homestake ... 15, 132, 170
Horsehead Creek ... 46
Hot Brook Canyon ... 112
Hot Springs, Arkansas ... 75
Hot Springs Herald ... 97
Hot Springs High School ... 109
Hot Springs Hotel (Hot Springs House) ... 21, 41, 105, 106
Hot Springs Star ... v, 77, 88, 97, 112, 114, 118
Hot Sulphur Springs, Virginia ... 75
Hull, Arundel C., Photographer ... 180

I

Iowa House ... 37, 79

J

Jackson, Eva ... 71
Jennings, Abbie ... 27
Jennings Avenue House ... 163
Jennings, Dr. Rudolph Dickenson (R. D.) ... 27, 41, 55, 62–63, 72, 112
Jennings, Mrs. R. D., Mattie (Curtiss) ... 27, 28, 41, 53–56, 59
Jenny, Prof. [Walter T.] ... 18
Jensen, C. L. (Chris) ... 39–40, 141
Joe Petty ... 22

K

Kansas City Daily Journal, newspaper ... 82
Keystone Cattle Company ... 52
Knowlton, W. H. (Walt) ... 144
Kohler, John, Judge ... 37

L

L7 Ranch ... 52
LaFleiche, William A. ... 63, 72
Lame Johnny Creek ... 52
Laramie Boomerang ... 97
Larive, Joe ... 20
Lead, South Dakota ... xviii, 15, 132, 169, 179
Lemmon, Ed ... 52, 71
Lewis and Clark ... 12
Lincoln Avenue ... 62, 86
Lincoln Hall ... 63, 85
Literary and Debating Society ... 63, 66, 71
Longhorns Bring Culture ... 52
Lower Town, Hot Springs ... 23, 28, 71, 107, 123

M

Map, modern Hot Springs ... 198
Map, ranches and brands ... 52
Martin, Eben W. ... 48–49, 142
Marty, George ... 67
Marty, Henry ... 50, 112
Marty, Joe ... 93, 95
Marty, Stu, photograph ... 95
Messiah craze ... 115–118
Methodist church ... xviii, 40, 85, 86
Miles, General (Nelso A.) ... 116, 118

Minnekahta Avenue ... 20, 29, 30, 71, 79, 101, 107, 127, 146
Minnekahta Bathhouse ... 105
Minnekahta Block ... 106, 113–114, 177
Minnekahta Falls ... 19
Minnekahta Hotel ... 76, 79, 102, 110
Minnekahta, South Dakota ... 29, 36, 38, 40, 42, 44–45, 50, 52, 53, 56, 58, 59, 63, 69, 70, 72, 75, 146
Mrs. A. S. Stewart ... 75

N

National Heights ... 16
Newell, South Dakota ... 97
Nichols Cancer Sanitarium ... 128–129
North Western Railroad ... 69
Nye, Bill ... 97

O

Oar Lock Ranch ... 52
Oelrichs, Harry ... 43
Oelrichs, South Dakota ... 43–44, 50, 52, 121–122, 144, 145
Oglala Sioux ... 17, 120. *See also* Sioux
Oregon Trail ... 17
Our Lady of Lourdes ... 41. *See also* Sisters' Hospital

P

Parkman, Francis ... 16–17
Parsons, Ed ... 52
Petty, Edmund (Ted) ... 23, 146
Petty, Joe ... 22, 28
Petty Livery Barn ... 29, 76
Philadelphia ... 52
Pierce, Fred ... 55
Pierre, South Dakota ... 73, 140
Pine Ridge Indian camp ... 116–117
Pioneer Museum, Hot Springs, SD ... 68, 102, 147, 176
Plum Creek ... 68
Powell, Al ... 50
Presbyterian Church ... 110–111
Protestant Service ... 84

R

Rapid City Journal, newspaper ... 114
Rapid City, South Dakota ... xxv, 15, 59, 118, 122, 164

Red Cloud, Chief ... 30, 31, 56
Reno, Ludlow B. ... 21–22, 31
Reno, Will ... 31–32
Richer, John G. (Johnnie) ... 52, 71, 77, 142
Riordan, A. W. (Archie) ... 141
River Avenue ... 29, 38, 61, 71, 77, 100, 132, 136
Robinson, U. S. G. (Grant) ... 143
Roe, Charley ... 50
Root, W. W. ... 112
Ross, Horatio N. ... 17

S

Scenic Road ... 22
Schatz, August ... 52
Scribner's Magazine ... xxiv, 138, 148
Searles, Rev. Jesse D. ... 40
Seven Sisters Range ... 125, 130, 137, 147
Seventh Street ... 77, 93, 136
Sheperd, Jim (Old Shep) ... 45
Shep's Canyon ... 45, 119
Shirt Tail Canyon bunch ... 94
Sidney-Deadwood Stage Line ... 29
Siloam Bathhouse ... 130
Sioux ... 7–8, 10, 12, 17, 31, 56, 75, 115, 118–119, 136. *See also* Oglala Sioux
Sisters' Hospital ... 39, 41
Sitting Bull ... 120
Sixth Street ... 38
Smith, G. Carroll ... 143
South Dakota State Soldiers' Home ... 101–102, 136–137, 164
Spearfish, South Dakota ... 15, 132
Stanley, Mrs. W. H. (Blanche) ... 38, 75
Stanley, W. H. (Ward) ... 67
Stetter, John G. ... 88
Stewart, Blanche ... 75, 99
Stewart, Charles ... 99
Stewart, Dr. Alexander S. ... 26–30, 38, 63, 69, 71–72, 74, 77, 100, 102, 105, 108, 112, 123, 131, 137, 140
Stewart, Harry ... 99
Stewart, Mrs. A. S. ... 30, 38, 59, 75, 100
Sturgis Record, newspaper ... 108
Sturgis, South Dakota ... 15, 56, 179

T

TAN ranch ... 50

3rd Infantry ... 57
13th Cavalry ... 57
Thornby, Col. W. J. ... 18, 20, 27
Thunder Hawk ... 122–123
Tillotson, Claude ... 65
Trimmer, George ... 74, 131, 137
Trimmer, George and Mary ... 22–24
Trimmer's Grove ... 23
Turner, George ... 22, 24, 52

U

Union Depot ... 113, 126
Union Pacific Railroad ... 17, 180
Upper Town ... 106, 107

V

Valley Irrigator, newspaper ... 97

W

warm springs ... 2, 5, 7, 15, 26, 53, 101, 112, 138, 145
Warm Springs ... 7. *See also* Wi-wi-la-kahta
West, Shorty ... 52
WG Flat ... 52, 160
WG Ranch ... 52, 61, 142
Wilson, Clifford ... 96
Wilson, Edith ... 96
Wilson, S.E. (Stephen Eugene) ... 96
Wind Cave ... 34–36, 47, 99, 141
Wi-wi-la-kahta ... 7. *See also* Warm Springs
Wounded Knee ... 120
Wyatt, Mrs. W. F. ... 119
Wyatt, W. F. (Bill) ... 46, 92, 93, 95, 119

Z

Z Bell Ranch ... 52
Zither Dick (Richard Bassel) ... 61–62

Points of Interest

Hot Brook Canyon	1
Chautauqua (Park)	2
Evans Plunge (Lakota group of springs)	3
Evans Heights	4
Courthouse	5
Gibson Hotel (Flat Iron Guest Suites)	6
Battle Mountain / National Heights	7
Battle Mountain Sanitarium (VA)	8
Union Depot	9
Minnekahta Block	10
Evans Hotel	11
Sisters' Hospital	12
Gillespie Hotel	13
Dr. Alexander Stewart's log house	14
Indian Bathtub / Hot Springs House, Hotel, Minnekahta Bathhouse	15
State Soldiers' Home	16
Country Club	17
Black Hills College (Hot Springs High School)	18
Fargo-Dickover Building (Bering Building)	19
Hot Springs School (Pioneer Museum)	20
Catholican / Seven Sisters Range / Siloam Springs Bathhouse	21

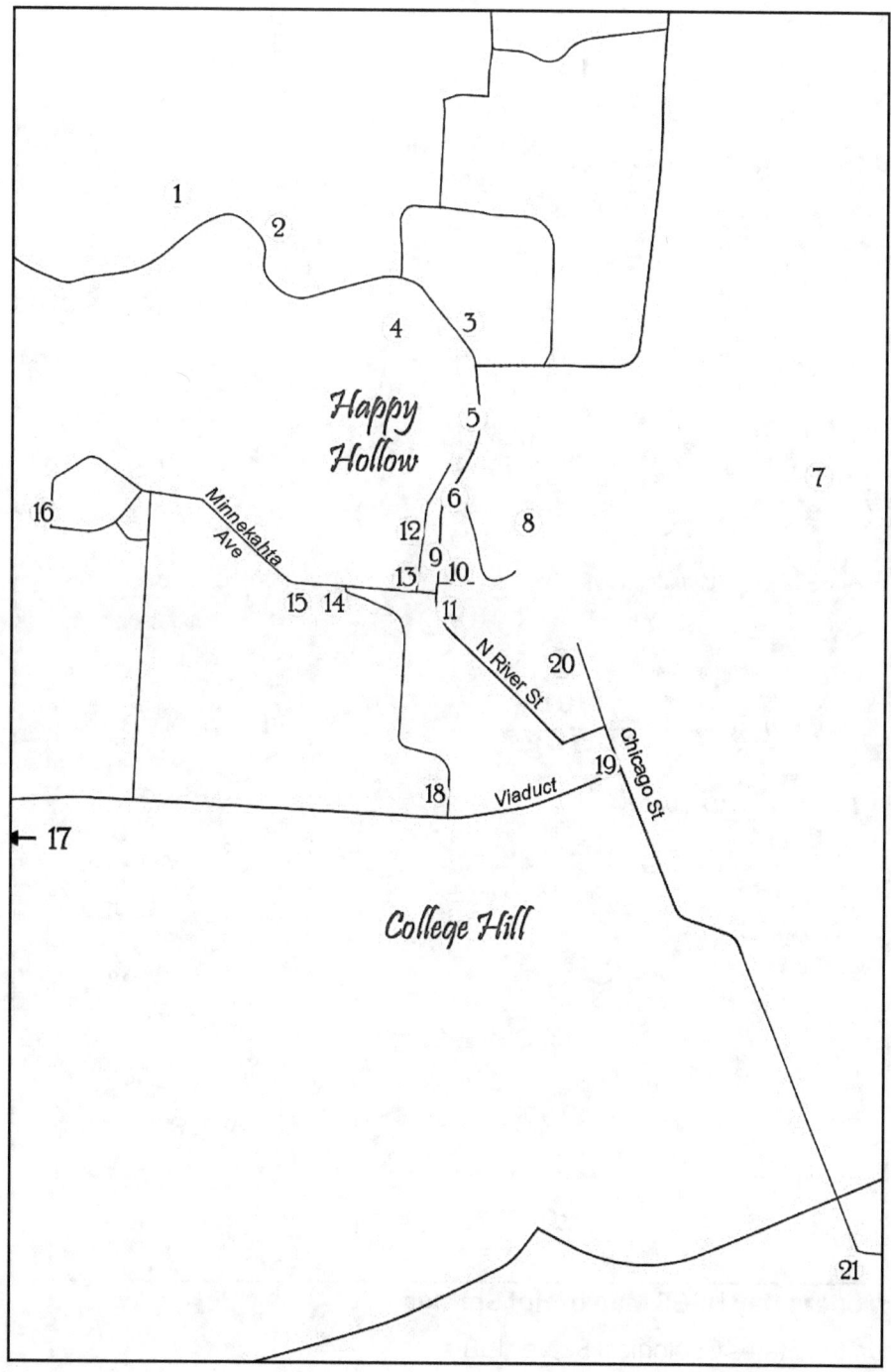

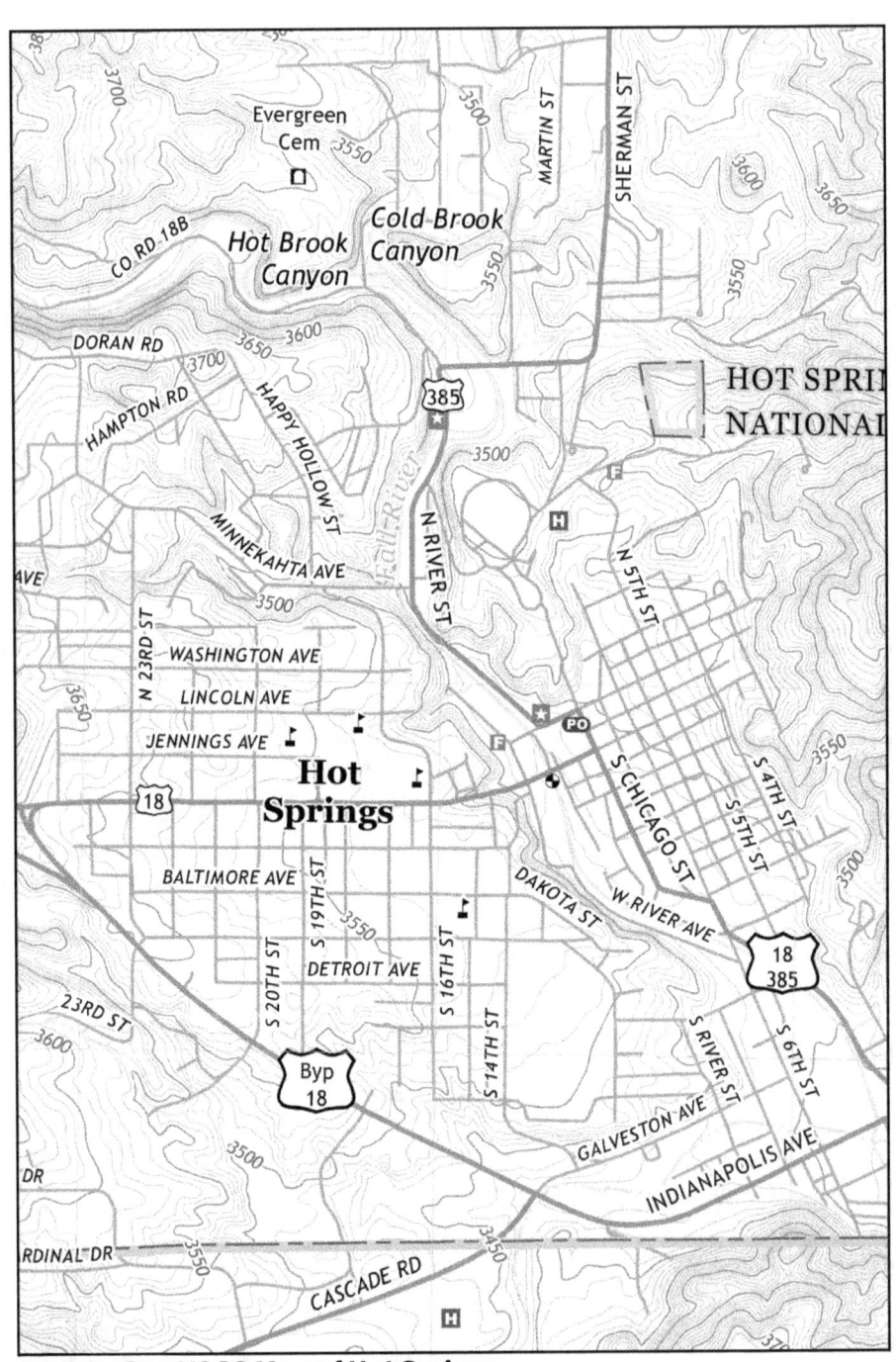

Modern Day USGS Map of Hot Springs
United States Geological Survey 1984

www.ingramcontent.com/pod-product-compliance
Lightning Source LLC
Chambersburg PA
CBHW051942290426
44110CB00015B/2079